"Beth Hildebrand's *The Art of Struggling* is a unique blend of personal experiences, Scripture, prayers, and artistic expressions. She will speak directly to your soul with her words and the exercises she suggests for you, the reader. It is hard for me to believe that this is her first book and I know it won't be her last. Put this on your list as a must read!"

† JANE ALBRIGHT, Former Head NCAA Women's Basketball Coach, Owner of Things Above Book Store

"Beth Hildebrand offers a compassionate and caring course of action to help fellow travelers navigate life's stormy weather with confident hope in *The Art of Struggling*. Drawing on the wisdom that is both ancient and profoundly relevant, I sensed Beth standing at the door praying for readers embarking on their journey."

† FIL ANDERSON, Author of *Running on Empty*

"Beth's insights from the Lord shake me to my core. Her writing creates beautiful and intimate moments with God of surrender, trust, and fulfillment. With each turn of the page, Beth's words bore deeper into my soul to draw me into more intimate conversations with the God who fully loves me. Her personal insights on how trials in the daily grind of life impact our soul resonate with me profoundly. Her words etch themselves in my heart in a way that causes me to yearn for more vulnerability before the Lord. This is a book I can come back to season after season to remind myself of how God beautifully weaves the art of struggling into the tapestry of who we are as His beloved workmanship and masterpiece."

† MARVITA FRANKLIN, Writer and Leader Development Coach and Author of *He Makes All Things Beautiful: God's Transformation of Our Emotional Wounds, Scars, and Brokenness*

"An excellent, biblically grounded guide for anyone, any time. Because we all suffer, we can relate to the stories shared by Beth Hildebrand with transparency and authenticity. This work prompts devotion and worship, with interactive exercises for deeper meaning and application. This will definitely be added to my collection of resources for those seeking to improve their mental health and well-being!"

"If you're weighed down by the all-too-real challenges of life and you need a friend to come near, let me introduce you to Beth Hildebrand. She empathizes with your struggle and desires to help you find a way through to fullness of life once again. She's traversed darkness, both literal loss of sight and the dark night of the soul. But she didn't stay there. She found a way through the loss and betrayal, and you can too. When the mountain is too high, it's best to go through instead of over, but you need someone to show you the way. Join Beth on a gentle journey, full of grace and mercy for your hurting heart that longs to be mended. She's the friend you've been looking for."

"As an artist and storyteller, Beth warmly invites us to embrace and exercise our right brain so suffering and imagination would become deeper companions. She reminds us that the lost poetic art of lament is a call to release our brokenness and return to God's healing kindness. Get ready as her paradigm of scripture, story, prayer, art, and song helps sharpen our belief that God views us as His masterpiece. You will feel compelled to create new expressions with your hands, heart, and voice—imagine that!"

"What a beautiful respite. We all struggle, and Beth helps us to look at our struggles in new ways. She is a wonderful leader and a kind guide of time with our Lord through these pages. As an artist, I appreciate the uniqueness in which Beth walks us between prayer, stories, reflecting and expressing while using our senses and creativity on our journey to persevere through struggles. This book gives you tools and hope!"

† JENNIFER UECKERT, Artist @Studio JRU and
a published write for (in)courage-a DaySpring community

"The Art of Struggling is an honest and encouraging look at many kinds of struggles. Beth writes with a genuine and loving heart, and I trust that readers will be encouraged by her stories and practical ideas for how they, too, might survive and thrive during seasons of struggle. I also appreciate how she's woven scripture and glimpses into her relationship with God throughout the book."

† DR. SHANNON WARDEN, Author, Counselor,
and Associate Professor of Counseling

The Art of Struggling, by Beth N. Hildebrand

First published in the United States of America
April 2022 by PathGuide Publishing

www.bethhildebrand.com

Unless otherwise indicated, all Scripture quotations are taken from *The Holy Bible*, New Living Translation, © 1996, 2004, 2007, by Tyndale House Foundation. Used by permission of Tyndale House Publishers, Inc., Carol Stream, Illinois 60188. All rights reserved. Scripture quotations marked NIV are taken from the New International Version. ©1988, 1989, 1990, 1991. Used by permission of Tyndale House Publishers.

ISBN paperback: 979-8-9857450-0-9

ISBN eBook: 979-8-9857450-1-6

Cover design by Beth Hildebrand

Interior design and formatting by Nelly Murariu at PixBeeDesign.com

THE *Art* OF STRUGGLING

Finding Hope When
It Feels Like Your
World's Falling Apart

BETH N. HILDEBRAND

CONTENTS

Before You Begin

Dear reading friend,

The Art of Struggling was intently written to guide your soul from the black, white, and grays of struggling into a life filled with beautiful colors of hope. As you read this book, you'll discover its uniqueness as you participate in it with me.

What does that mean? This book is designed so you can take your own time and work through it at your own pace. No rule says you need to get through each chapter in one sitting. I recommend you do not do that. Instead, let these pages create a space for you to release your thoughts, feelings, and emotions, whatever they may be. I want to stroll with you on this journey as we cultivate the spiritual discipline of how to struggle well with hope. These chapters are guided times with the Lord because when you're struggling or suffering, it's hard to know where to start when it comes to connecting with God. Peter, Jesus' disciple, tells us that you and I are God's *special possession Who calls us out of darkness into His wonderful light.* (1 Peter 2:9) We belong to God, who calls us extraordinary. Sometimes though, it takes a little guidance and encouragement to live out that Truth.

This book is also a tool you can use in a time of personal joy and contentment as a reminder of God's grace and compassion for you or as a resource when you're walking through a struggling season with someone you care about or love. It can also be a resource to help create a spiritual habit of time with the Lord.

Here's what you can expect in each chapter:

  † *A beginning pre-written prayer*: I know, sometimes when we're in a funk, it can be hard to pray on our own. Guided prayer is good for anyone at any season in life, and these

specifically chosen prayers relate to specific situations you may be experiencing. After reading the prayer, take a little time to sit still and reflect on the words of that prayer quietly. Past and present Bible teachers and authors wrote these prayers.

† *Scripture*: Throughout each chapter, verses are God-breathed and written for you. I recommend reading them slowly, meditating on them (read them more than once), so the Truth can take root in your soul. It's a good practice to stay in the Word daily, and these verses are to assure you of God's promises for your life.

† *A story*: There is a relatable story to encourage you. It includes a personal story, how a person in the Bible experienced a similar struggle, and how God redeems us from them. You are not the only one. As you go through this journey, may you feel God's warm, strong hands take hold of your hand and place it on His chest so you can feel His heart pounding with deep affection for you. Because He does. (Dane Ortlund, *Gentle and Lowly: The Heart of Christ for Sinners and Sufferers*)

(As you read this book, I suggest getting a notebook, journal book, or even a sketchbook to record your thoughts and expressions, and you'll see why below.)

† *Personal Reflection*: There are two questions to ask yourself reflectively. Answer them at your speed. Resist the urge to answer them quickly with one-word responses. Instead, ask your soul what you honestly think when asked those questions. Included is additional Scripture for you to read and reflect on. Read it slowly and prayerfully (maybe read one of them for a few days, marinading on it—which is why it's hard to call this book a devotional. Consider it a discipline).

† *Personal Expression*: This is your invitation to exercise the right side of your brain. Here's an avenue for you to worship God through creativity. *You do not need to be artistic or crafty,*

I promise! There are various ways to express your feelings, and I dare you to join me as we use our different senses to experience God in a new way.

† *A Song*: I once read that music is a piece of art that goes in the ears and straight to the heart. Each chapter has a suggested song from all different genres—another opportunity to be present with God and rest in His promises for you.

† *A Closing Prayer*: These are Scripture prayers where different verses in the Bible are hemmed together into prayer. Again, this is another opportunity to meditate on the Word of God.

Specially designed for you, this book is a respite from your struggles. I pray that these pages offer a place of refuge and rest where you'll feel safe and loved.

Introduction

One tear dropped from my eye and slowly rolled down the side of my face as I stood in front of the painting. All I could see in this masterpiece that hung on the wall were dark green, gray, and almost black blurs. I don't know if the blurry vision was from my tears or my new reality. Three months earlier, I had an unexpected brain surgery that resulted in a vision loss. Growing up living down the road from the North Carolina Museum of Art, it had become my place of refuge even though I was too young to realize it. As a teenager, I volunteered there and dreamed of being an artist one day.

Feeling cooped up during recovery, I visited the art museum for a change of atmosphere one afternoon. I meandered to one of my favorite paintings—*Bridal Veil Falls: Yosemite* by Albert Bierstadt. Standing in front of the painting, I saw only half of it—I had lost almost all my vision to the right.

That moment was one of great sorrow and great joy. I grieved this significant and permanent loss of vision, yet at the same time, I was grateful that I still had half of my sight. I mourned my partial blindness yet felt joyful that the beautiful spectrums of colors were still visible to me.

Now, many years later, I'm finally learning that more than likely, in our various life experiences, "great sorrow and great joy are often seen to be parts of the same experience."[1] Both can welcome tears, both emerge from the soul, and both of those emotions matter. The difference is that joy is a choice we must make, and sorrow is not an experience we choose.

---

1 Henri Nouwen, *Here and Now* (New York, Crossroad Publishing Company, 1994)

More than likely, you have faced struggling seasons in your life or know someone who has. You might be in the middle of one right now. The reality is, is that we live in a broken world. And yet! When we invite Jesus to dwell in our lives and souls, we're enabled to persevere through trials and suffering. With Jesus, He gives us the ability to experience a deep joy even in sorrow.

Since my surgery, I've had some practice of living with struggling and joy simultaneously. The day before my surgery, my surgeon did not tell me I had a chance of losing my vision, but he did tell me that I would probably struggle with depression. I assumed that meant only temporarily as I recovered, and I was too young and scared to ask if my assumption was correct. Unfortunately, it was incorrect, and I've struggled with it on and off ever since. I've also learned that brain trauma, such as surgery, can cause life-long side effects—including depression and mental struggles. Yet, I've learned that it's become part of the overall masterpiece God continues to develop in me.

The National Psychiatric Association 2020 Mental Health Study shows that mental health conditions, like depression and anxiety, impact one in five adults—almost 47 million people in America."[2] And even more concerning, the number of youth (12–17 years) suffering from a mental disorder increased 99,000 since 2019— just one year.[3] Alarmingly, many more don't admit to suffering or struggling because we think it isn't popular (secularly and in churches across the hills, valleys, and mountains of this country). Today as I write this, I confess to you that I've been one of those 47 million people who have suffered from this challenging aversion. Several years ago, I would have never admitted to my family that I struggled with depression, much less created a book relating to it for anyone to read.

---

2 The State of Mental Health in America" Mental Health America, Inc. 2021, www.mhanational.org/issues/state-mental-health-america
3 "Prevalence Date 2021." Mental Health America, Inc. 2021, https://mhanational.org/issues/2021/mental-health-america-youth-data

Culturally, now more than ever, many people have resources at the tips of their fingers to help with mental health struggles, yet we continue to struggle with the stigma and shame that inhibit us from getting help. In addition, we're afraid of losing the respect of people in our village or community. Eugene Peterson describes that well when he wrote, "It is difficult to find anyone in our culture who will respect us when we suffer."[4]

I am not an expert on psychology or brain science. My degree is in art and English, not science and medicine. But I know from experience what it's like to live in a state of grief, isolation, doubtfulness, and anxiety. I've lived seasons of depression on and off since I was a college student when I had brain surgery. So while I don't know all the facts that come from intense research and study about the brain, I can speak from what I have lived. Mental health struggles are real, and you are not alone. I can also tell you that even if you've been a Christ-follower—whether for a week or many years—it doesn't prevent you from suffering.

In this book, we'll see how Scripture is full of stories cover-to-cover about people God used to show and teach us about struggling. Their stories are old, but their struggles are just as present today as they were alive. Here, we're going to search deeper into people's lives and the real-life struggles they lived with, just like we do.

God's Book is a beautiful masterpiece of redemption and love. Nevertheless, nowhere in Scripture does it say we're going to have an easy life here on this side of the Kingdom of God. Paul wrote clearly to the Jesus seekers and followers in Rome then and to us today.

> *We also celebrate in seasons of suffering because we know that when we suffer, we develop endurance, which shapes our characters. When our characters are refined, we learn what it means to hope and anticipate God's goodness. And hope will*

---

4   Eugene Peterson, *A Long Obedience in the Same Direction: Discipleship in an Instant Society*, (Downers Grove, IL: InterVarsity Press, 2000) p. 138

never fail to satisfy our deepest need because the Holy Spirit
that was given to us has flooded our hearts with God's love.

† (**Romans 5:3-5 The Voice**)

A few paragraphs later in his letter, Paul also writes,

"And since we are his children, we are his heirs. In fact, together
with Christ we are heirs of God's glory. But if we are to share
his glory, we must also share his suffering." † (**Romans 8:17**)

And yet!

"Yet what we suffer now is nothing compared to the glory he
will reveal to us later." † (**Romans 8:18**)

Sharing in Christ's suffering can be great sorrow. Yet, the grace
and gentleness He gives us *now* will be revealed as we go through
our daily lives, never giving up our hope. But we must pay attention so we can also experience the great joy He pours over us.

That afternoon in the art museum many years ago, staring at
Bierstadt's masterpiece, my eyes turned to the right so I could
see the rest of the painting. Bierstadt called the Yosemite area the
"Garden of Eden." He portrayed that in his work, especially in *The
Bridal Veil*. The majestic power of the bright, white water falling
over the granite tower reflects God's majesty. The radiant sunshine
appears to be breaking through dark clouds, casting light into the
deep valley of the detailed rushing river, large rocks, evergreen
trees, and tiny deer. It reminded me how Jesus is the Light of the
world who shines light into the dark valleys in life's journey.

Even with my lack of complete vision, I was able to see that to
create dimension in a painting or drawing, shading is necessary
by using different hues of dark colors. Preventing objects from
looking flat and lacking depth, there must be light *and* negative
space or darkness. A masterpiece needs dark shades to accentuate
the beauty of the painting. You are God's masterpiece. As the Artist,
He uses the light and dark values in your life to give His masterpiece depth, making the final piece vibrant and breathtakingly
beautiful.

Jesus, and others, did not live a life free of darkness and suffering as we will read in Scripture. Great sorrow—Jesus had to suffer, feeling abandoned and bearing the weight of our sins as he died on the cross. Yet, he arose from the dark tomb alive on the third day—great joy! And when we hold onto the *hope found in Jesus* through his resurrection, we too can experience great joy—even as we struggle.

If there's anything I want to emphasize to you, it's that when you're struggling, stay in touch with Jesus. I know it can be a challenge, especially when it feels like He's so far away and you're alone, but if you don't give up, you'll be disciplining yourself in the holy practice of suffering *well*. Like praying, times of solitude, rest, meditating on Scripture—all examples Jesus gave us—suffering while fellowshipping with hope and joy in the Lord is yet another spiritual discipline to train ourselves to depend on Him more and draw us even closer to Him. We'll practice that together in the chapters to come as we experience the beautiful art of living with both struggles and joy.

May you choose joy amidst the struggles. May you live with hope in the thick of life's troubles. May you know that you know that you know that you are Creator God's splendid masterpiece.

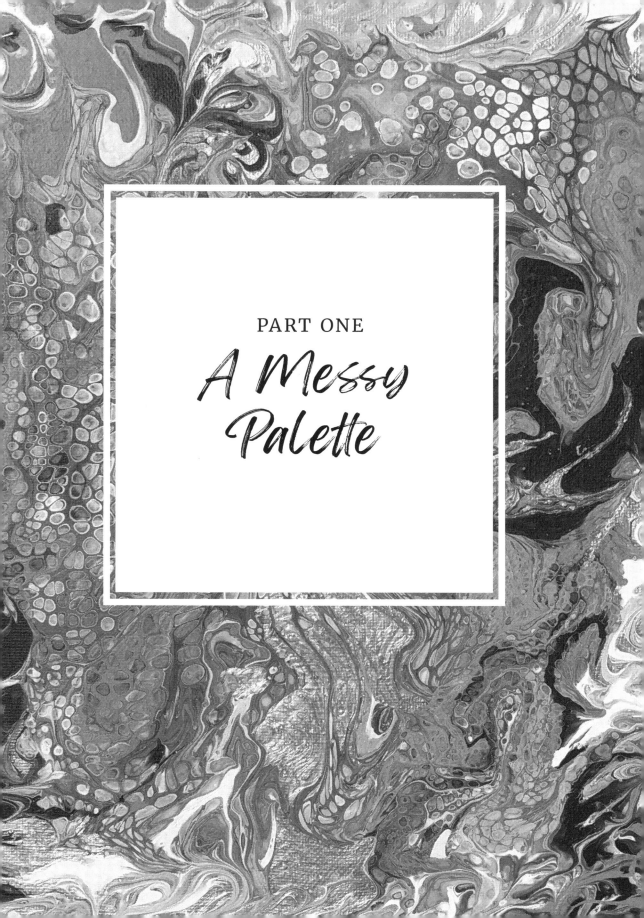

PART ONE

A Messy
Palette

CHAPTER 1

I'm Blinds

Opening Prayer

Here I am, O God, humbly yours, lifting up my heart to you, before whom all created things are as dust and mist. You are hidden behind the curtain of our limited sight and hearing, incomprehensible in your greatness, mysterious in your almighty power; yet here am I, speaking to you with the familiarity of a child to a parent, a friend to a friend. If I could not speak to you like this, then I would indeed be without hope in the world.

† **John Baillie**, *A Diary of Private Prayer: A Devotional Classic*[1]

"So, we don't look at the troubles we can see now; rather, we fix our gaze on things that cannot be seen. For the things we see now will soon be gone, but the things we cannot see will last forever."

† **(2 Corinthians 4:18)**

Story

It was March 3, 1993

I lie uncomfortably on a silvery-shiny, hard and cold surgery board covered by the dense weight of layers of white, cotton

---

1 John Baillie. A Diary of Private Prayer: A Devotional Classic, updated and revised by Susanna Wright (New York: Scribner, A Division of Simon & Schuster, Inc 1949) p. 35

nkets. I heard the squeaky sound from the wheels carrying me down the sterile hall. My eyes were closed as I whispered, "Be strong and courageous," quoting Joshua 1:9 in the Bible over and over, not knowing what I'd see when I opened them again.

In the operating room, my head was cut and peeled open. For eight hours that day, doctors worked tediously de-tangling the twisted capillaries in my brain to stop my blood from clotting. A couple of days later, when I opened my eyes, I mainly saw black in the late morning hour. Unintentionally, a small nerve was clipped during the surgery clipped, causing me to lose half of my vision.

My world was spinning. Literally. I had terrible vertigo, and it took me another day or so to realize the reason I had it was because I had lost a significant part of my sight. I was trying to find balance as I grappled with my loss, wondering and praying it would come back.

I was very thankful for recovering as well as I did. Now, many years later, I've had no more seizures that could have caused a severe aneurism, which was the goal of the surgery. Some other life-long challenges arose from it, though, as I mentioned in the Introduction, especially my vision loss.

Days passed, and then months. I had to adapt to this void I had never experienced. My eyes had to work extra hard. I had to look to the right more. Several months later, after a few appointments at the optometrist, I was told a small fraction of vision thankfully did return, but it was all that would ever come back. I lost almost all my right peripheral vision.

The 20 years before my surgery, I lived with a similar lack of vision. My second home for the first 18 years of my life was the church on the corner, at the highest hill in the capital city of North Carolina. As my mom practiced the organ in the sanctuary a few days a week, my sister and I played hide and seek in the pews. The staircase on the way to the choir room was where I had my first kiss. Sunday evening was youth group that I rarely missed, and each summer, for one hot and humid week, we'd go on a local mission trip to repair homes for the needy.

Even though being raised in a church, I had a spiritual, visual impairment. I read the Bible occasionally and paid attention to small parts of some sermons, but I didn't really notice Jesus in my life. Then, on February 4, 1993, when I found out I had to have brain surgery, about ten students at my college's Fellowship of Christian Athletes meeting put their hands on me and prayed over and for me. After that night, I saw life in a new way. It looked different because I was looking from the foot of the cross with a new set of eyes. The veil that made it hard for me to see God's Light during my youth had been lifted by God's grace. Now, I could clearly see His love for me and felt the peace of His presence.

During the 27 days of waiting until my surgery, God put people in my life—friends from near and far and people I had never met before, who gave me Scripture to encourage me and teach me what it means to have a relationship with God. He became real to me. I began writing. Prayer had an entirely new meaning to me. I had a faithful vision with new hope accompanied by confident peace. I went into that operating room confident that the Lord was with me.

Since my surgery, though, I sometimes wonder, what good was I supposed to gain from losing my vision? All it seems to do is worry my husband. I miss having something beautiful suddenly "catch my eye" through the window beside me riding down the road. At the movies or a meeting, I need to sit to the right side of the room to see as much as possible to the left. I'm a slow reader.

I'm aware of it every day, yet at the same time, I'm not. I live with it. It's become my norm to be partially blind, and through the years after my surgery, I had allowed it to become my norm to be partially blind to the vision God saw in me. There were days where doubt, worry, fear, and self-pity appeared and reappeared and put a dark veil over my eyes, making the beauty of God's vision of me challenging to see. Maybe you understand this too: some seasons in life can be a challenge not to lose sight of our roles in God's Story.

Several years ago, God started showing me how to see things differently. On a brisk autumn morning walk, the cool air that blew over my face opened my eyes to see the tips of leaves start to become displays of art on neighborhood trees. I sat on the sofa when I got home, welcoming the morning sun. Then, I opened my Bible to read Luke 18:35-43, about Jesus healing a blind man. I don't know how many times I'd read that and thought, "Oh, that's another moment of Jesus' life—a good story."

"He came to the outskirts of Jericho. A blind man was sitting beside the road asking for handouts. When he heard the rustle of the crowd, he asked what was going on. They told him, "Jesus, the Nazarene is going by."

He called, "Jesus, Son of David, have mercy on me!"

Those ahead of Jesus told the man to be quiet, but he only yelled all the louder, "Son of David! Mercy, have mercy on me!"

Jesus stopped and asked that the man be brought to him. When he came near, Jesus asked, "What do you want from me?"

The blind man said, "Master, I want to see again."

Jesus said, "Go ahead—see again! Your faith has saved and healed you!" The healing was instant: He looked up, seeing—and then followed Jesus, glorifying God. Everyone in the street joined in, shouting praise to God."

Why had it never dawned on me that I'm that blind man?

I call out to God the same things the blind man called out to Jesus. Some days I quietly say, with a whisper of hope, "Master,

I want to see again," and other days, I cry out to God, "Mercy! Please have mercy on me! Why did my vision have to be taken from me? Why haven't You given it back to me? I want to be normal and see as I did before my surgery!"

Maybe there's something you call out to God similar to the blind man. "Master, please have mercy on me! Why did you take my husband away from me and leave me alone with two young children? Why haven't you given me the ability to live without chronic pain every day? Master, why can't I find a spouse? Why has my child gone wayward? Master, have mercy on me and relieve me from struggling with this addiction! Why won't You heal me from anxiety?"

After reading those verses in Luke, I felt as if Jesus was looking at me, saying, "*I don't want you to be normal and see things the way the world does. If you can have faith like that blind man and like you did when you first fell in love with Me 27 days before your surgery, you'll see things in a beautiful, new way. I want you to focus on the things you* cannot *see*."

Look beyond the outside appearances. Reach to the unseen where there are broken hearts, a longing for peace, and souls yearning for wholeness.

Paul painted a beautiful picture with words in his second letter to the Corinthians about the reason why we're to focus on what we're not able to see:

> "*You see, the short-lived pains of this life are creating for us an eternal glory that does not compare to anything we know here. So, we do not set our sight on what we can see with our eyes. All of that is fleeting; it will eventually fade away. Instead, we focus on the things we cannot see, which live on and on.*"
>
> **† (2 Corinthians 4:17–18)**

God can use our impairments, struggles, and challenges to remind us of His presence in our lives. They can be constant prompts to keep us aware of His grace and goodness. Do not lose your God-given vision of the work of art He created in you. Keep your eyes focused on our unseen God all around us, no matter what your actual vision is.

I can now see that He puts specific visions and dreams in *our* hearts and callings in *our* lives so *we* can see the miraculous ways God works in and through us. Because the Holy Spirit lives inside of us, we're given the ability to see into the hearts and hindrances of people around us. We can then help them set their eyes on what cannot be seen—our invisible God who is alive and continues to do His purposeful works.

While our physical or mental struggles can remain, we can gain a new vision spiritually.

Honestly, it was more than worth it if it took losing my vision to find Jesus. He freely gives us a new sight that no person or thing can take away from us. Sometimes our lives can become foggy, or we have difficulty seeing the reasons, but God never loses His perfect sight of His beloved children whom He beholds with mercy and love.

Personal Reflections

The blind man said, "Master, I want to see again." What do you want to say to Jesus? Fill in the blank. "Master, I want to ...."

List some earthly things that you find yourself setting your sight on that will one day fade away. Then list some things that you can focus on that you cannot see that can give you hope.

Additional Scripture: 2 Corinthians 4:7–18, Colossians 1:15–20, Mark 10:46–52

Personal Expressions

God created us to have five senses: sight, taste, touch, smell and hear. We often take them for granted. Research has proven that paying attention to our senses helps calm our minds, increase our compassion, improve our immune system, improve sleep, decrease anxiety and stress, and make us happier.[2]

Here's an exercise to help take your mind off of concerns and improve your mental health.

Observe five things you can see. Then, look around, paying attention to the things you don't often notice around you.

Notice 4 things you can feel. Rub your hands over textured things in your current environment or what you're wearing.

Listen to the 3 sounds you hear. They can be close or in the distance. There are sounds we don't often notice because of other distracting noisiness.

What are 2 scents you smell? For example, can you smell the scent from a candle, what's cooking in the kitchen— or a smelly trashcan?

Focus on 1 thing you taste. Is it a sip of your coffee, a sweet treat of dark chocolate, or the lingering taste of garlic from your most recent meal?

Practice this as often as you'd like or when you need to calm your mind.

🔊 **Listen to *Be Thou My Vision* by Audrey Assad**

---

2 Victoria Schmidgall. "Mindful Monday: Try the 'Five Senses' Mindfulness Exercise." *The University of Vermont Medical Center* 29 January 2018, https://medcenterblog. uvmhealth.org/wellness/physical/mindfulness-mindful-monday-exercise

Closing Prayer

God, You are the eternal King, the unseen one who never dies; You alone are God who created everything in the heavenly realms and on earth. You made the things I can see and the things I can't see—such as thrones, kingdoms, rulers, and authorities in the unseen world. Everything was created through You and for You. When I cry out to You, "Lord, have mercy on me!," please hear my plead. Help me to see the way You see. All honor and glory to You forever and ever!

† (1 Timothy 1:17, Colossians 1:16, Luke 18:38)

CHAPTER 2

I'm Exhausted

Opening Prayer

Father, we ask for clarity, but we understand that's not your highest priority. Draw us closer in our confusion, our doubt, and our questions. May we not work so hard to get rid of those things. Rather, may we let the questions and uncertainties pave the way to you. Help us to know when to say yes and when to say no. Give us the courage to quit when it's time. We declare you are always enough. We believe it. Help us in our unbelief. Amen.

† Emily P. Freeman, *The Next Right Thing*[1]

Pray like this:

Dear Father, always near us,

may your name be treasured and loved,

may your rule be completed in us—

may your will be done here on earth

in just the way it is done in heaven.

Give us today the things we need today,

and forgive us our sins and impositions on you,

---

1 Emily P. Freeman, *The Next Right Thing: A Simple, Soulful Practice for Making Life Decisions,* (Grand Rapids, MI Revel Publishing, 2019) p. 114

as we are forgiving all who in any way offend us.

Please don't put us through trials,

but deliver us from everything bad.

Because you are the one in charge,

And you have all the power,

And the glory too is all yours—forever—

which is just the way we want it.

Amen (or, Whoopie)!

† **(Matthew 6:9–13[2])**

Story

For several years, part of my husband and my morning rituals is taking our miniature schnauzer for an early morning walk. The red cardinals, orange-bellied robins, wrens, and mourning doves welcome us to the new day when we step outside. One of my favorite birds, though, is the bluebird, and throughout each year, we enjoy watching them in our yard.

One late winter morning, all bundled in winter coats and gloves, we reached the end of our driveway and noticed some commotion across the street on our neighbor's vehicle. A female bluebird was sitting on the roof of the truck, and at the side mirror, there was a male bluebird chirping profusely, fluttering and flapping his wings, and even flying into the side mirror.

That poor bird! He obviously saw his reflection, and it made me wonder if he thought he was at battle with another male bluebird to claim his territory. The birdhouse on a tree in our yard was several feet away, and that bluebird wasn't going to let any other bird stake a claim for it, even though it was just his reflection he fought. This winless battle went on for a few weeks!

---

2   Dallas Willard. *The Divine Conspiracy, Jesus' Master Class for Life: Participant's Guide* (Grand Rapids MI, Zondervan, 2010) p. 74 This is the Lord's Prayer Willard has paraphrased

To see if my hunch was correct, I googled and learned from a bird expert that, yes, it is due to domination and being territorial. But because of the bird's feathery feud, he becomes hugely exhausted or even hurt his delicate self to the point that he cannot do the more essential activities—finding food and tending to his nest.[3]

Observing those sweet, little bluebirds made me think about how we do ourselves the same thing. While we haven't physically rammed ourselves into a full-length mirror all day for a few weeks, we have overworked, overextended, and mentally overloaded ourselves to the point of exhaustion.

The oddity, though, is that it's normal, popular, and even expected to stay busy in today's culture. I can be at Target and see someone I know, and naturally, the first question is, "How are you?" The usual response is, "Busy! Work has been crazy; I'm chauffeuring the kids to rehearsals and practices, going to performances and games, along with volunteering at school and church. What about you?" "Oh, I'm busy, too." I cannot think of a time when someone said, "I have such a balanced life. I make time to rest, work is great, our kids have one activity one day a week, we have family dinner together every night, and I have long quiet time each day."

Another comment not heard very often these days when you ask someone how she's doing is this: "I'm spent, exhausted, and I kinda feel like I'm falling apart." That is usually what your friend is thinking in her head, but usually out of her mouth comes, "Oh, I'm busy but fine."

Why aren't we honest? Why do we overschedule ourselves? Why do we push ourselves so hard that we become ill and forced to rest because we didn't take the time to rest? It weakens or even damages relationships with ones we care about, or it can cause us to burn out mentally. Sometimes it's because climbing the ladder is a priority, or getting more likes and followers on social

3 Melissa Mayntz, 2020 The Spruce, accessed 6 March 2021 https://www.thespruce.com/stop-birds-attacking-windows-386449

media is a must to feel accepted. But, on the other hand, it could be because we're not good at saying, "No, not this time," or maybe, we're simply conforming to the norm because that's what everybody else does.

I know from life experiences that we *do* enjoy participating in activities, and we're not to be lazy. We enjoy our job (hopefully), spending time with our family, providing for our family, and volunteering, especially if it's for a good purpose or to do God's work. But if we allow our calendar to become too full, usually, one of the first things we drop is spending time with God and doing His work.

In the Bible, we can read about a man named Nehemiah, who gives us an excellent example of the importance of taking care of ourselves. He shows us the necessity to live with a rhythm. When Nehemiah worked as the cupbearer for the Persian king, the Holy Spirit pressed on his heart to rebuild the wall around the ruined Jerusalem after 125 years of war. When the king noticed that Nehemiah wasn't his usual happy self, he asked him what was wrong. Nehemiah told the king he wanted to rebuild the city in Judah where his father was buried.

The king gave his respected cupbearer, Nehemiah, his request, along with the bonus, which included a letter from the king stating Nehemiah would have protection on the way to Jerusalem, funding the wood to build the wall, and a place for him to live while it was under construction. The king granted him those, too, thanks to the "gracious hand of my God." (Nehemiah 2:8)

Once Nehemiah arrived at Jerusalem, he rounded up a group of people to help him build the wall after three days. Before long, they grew weary in their work. As The Message translation says, "The builders were pooped." These people were physically exhausted from the hard labor it took to build this two–and–a–half–mile–long wall around Jerusalem that was 40 feet high and over 8 feet thick.[4]

---

4   "Walls of Jerusalem." Wikipedia, 2021, https://en.wikipedia.org/wiki/Walls_of_ Jerusalem

I'd be worn out, too! They were not only physically tired, but they also carried anxiety and worry due to the threat of being murdered by the Samaritans as they worked. Nehemiah, though, picked up on this and prayed for the builders. After that, he designed a worthwhile, rotating plan: some worked, some kept watch for the enemy, and some ate and slept, and all of them wore weapons all the time until the wall was complete. God gave them the strength and protection they needed. God gave them the ability to complete the enormous project in only 52 days. They discovered that focusing on God and His purpose—to rebuild His holy city for His glory—gave them the strength they needed to complete it successfully.

While studying Nehemiah, I'm learning that it's OK to be worn out and exhausted when it comes to Kingdom work—just don't let it get to the point where you're burned out and ready to give up. Those are two different states of mind. God instructs us to practice Sabbath, which we'll read more about later in this book, and to take time to be still with Him in prayer and Bible reading consistently. Prayer and God's Word are restorative. Regular rest can give you more energy to do whatever needs to get accomplished. Use those powers to your advantage instead of repeatedly banging your head against a wall, fighting against yourself, thinking you can complete the things on your to-do list successfully and God's purpose single-handedly. When we over-extend our schedules, time of worship is often the first thing put to the side, which is how the enemy sneaks in to attack.

While I was learning about the bluebirds and their natural tendency to protect their territory, I also wanted to know how to prevent our bluebird from exhausting himself. One way is to cover the parked car mirror with a bag or cloth so it can no longer see its reflection. Another way to stop the attacks is to move the reflective object to a different location outside of his territory. Yes, those are good ways to help a bluebird, but let's make time to take care of ourselves, too. Then, we can be like Nehemiah and devise a tangible way to protect ourselves from exhaustion and even harm. Maybe you need to say "no" to something or someone. Perhaps you need to choose less than more. Maybe you need to give up something, borrow something, or hold on to something. God knows what that something is, so ask and listen.

We can beat ourselves to the point of exhaustion if we're not careful. We want to manage our time and decisions well. As believers, suffering will happen. Just like staying busy is a norm, struggling can be a norm, too, especially when we're exhausted.

Persevere, friend. Like Nehemiah, God's Spirit will give us the strength we need in tangible ways—we need to ask Him for them, though. God never tires or becomes weary. Instead, he sustains us and gives us the strength we need each day—just as He gives us our daily bread, which we ask Him for in the Lord's prayer. And let's take the time to enjoy the birds outside our windows.

Personal Reflections

Make some time for you to evaluate your physical and mental energy. For example, if you're struggling with exhaustion and weariness, what is causing you to feel that way? Is it something that can change? Is it necessary? Do you feel it's part of God's purpose in your life?

Right now, do you feel like you can be Nehemiah to someone, or you're like a builder exhausted and even fearful of the threat of being attacked? What do you think your next right thing should be? How can you make that happen?

Additional Scripture: Isaiah 40:28–31, Galatians 6:8–10, John 4:1–26

Personal Expressions

Schedule some time this week, an hour, for example, to de-clutter your mind and do a Scribble Coloring project that you'll find relaxing and soothing. You'll need your art journal or a blank piece of paper, some markers, colored pencils, or whatever mediums of colors you choose, and a dark-colored pen. With the marker or pen, draw lines all over the paper. They can be straight and curving lines but make sure they overlap and cross each other to form different abstract shapes. You just made your adult coloring design. Next, take your markers, crayon, colored pencils and fill in the abstract shapes with colors—pastel colors are soothing or bright colors make you happy! Remember, the process is more important than the product!

🔊 **Listen to** *Glory by Meek Squad*

Closing Prayer

Oh Lord, God of heaven, the great and awesome God, who keeps His covenant of love with those who love Him and obey His commands, let Your ear be attentive and Your eyes open to hear the prayer Your servant is praying before You, day and night. I confess the sins I committed against you. I have not obeyed the commands. I am Your servant whom You redeemed by Your great strength and Your mighty hand. O Lord, let Your ear be attentive to the prayer of this Your servant and to the prayer of Your servants who delight in revering Your name. Give Your servant success today by granting her favor. Amen

† **(parts of Nehemiah 1:5-10)**

CHAPTER 3

I'm Impatient

Opening Prayer

Lord, I'm so thankful that I can trust You, even in the most difficult and refining seasons of my life. Shape me. Purify me. Make me look more and more like You. I want to reflect You in all I say and do. In Jesus' Name, Amen. † **Lysa TerKeurst, Proverbs 31**[1]

The Lord's promises are pure, like silver refined in a furnace, purified seven times over. † **Psalm 12:6**

Story

More than likely, you're probably like me, having had a few emotional meltdowns in life. I've experienced a time or two when I've felt trapped in stress, or heightened frustrations triggered a verbal explosion due to a particular situation. Plenty of times, my temper has surged, my patience has gone up in flames, and I've yelled or cried out words I can't take back but wish I could.

We have meltdowns in all kinds of ways. Sometimes, they are spiritual. Spiritual meltdowns share some similarities with our emotional meltdowns—both emerge from the core of our souls, whether positive or negative. Emotional and spiritual meltdowns

---

1   Lysa TerKeurst. "The Blessing Found in the Fire." *Proverbs 31*, 25, July 2019, https://proverbs 31.org/read/devotions/full-post/2019/07/25/the-blessings-found-in-the-fire

can be due to a broken or a hardened heart. Both meltdowns might lead to tears. And God is present with us in both situations.

Spiritual meltdowns are not precisely like emotional meltdowns, though. While emotional breakdowns can cause regrets if tempers become out of control, spiritual meltdowns can cause renewal. Emotional meltdowns can keep us in bondage, while spiritual meltdowns can release us from bondage. Emotional explosions can be due to giving in to the wrong, yet God restores us to newness when we persevere through refinement.

Refinement is the purest example of the art of suffering and struggling. God's purpose of refining us is for us to become more like Himself—His image. The process of refining precious metals is a complex, slow process. First, they are often embedded in another rock. Then, the precious metals need to be mined. Once a nugget of gold extracts from a rock, it still contains other minerals, deposits, and particles, along with dirt. Removing the speckled impurities from the metal is necessary to see the pure, hidden beauty within.

The way to remove the impurities is through fire that causes the rocky formation to boil and melt. The impurities, or dross, rise to the pot's surface so the refiner can remove them. Once the dross is removed, the liquid gold continues to boil until it becomes pure—pure of any impurities. The refiner can see when it finally becomes pure when he looks into the liquid gold and sees his reflection, as clear as looking into a mirror.

That is spiritual refinement as well. God knows about our impurities, scuffs, and dirt embedded deep within and wants to remove them, even though sometimes the only way to do it is through discomfort and heat—and we become a 'hot-mess' as we sometimes hear people say. God can use the meltdown seasons in our lives to re-form us. Most of the time, we want a change in our lives to happen the way we want it to—quick and painless. We want God to magically snap His fingers so we can be instantly comfortable and happy. We don't like refinement because it can disembody our normalcy and dethrone our comfort.

Struggles in a relationship may raise bitterness and unforgiveness to the surface and might also make way for forgiveness to take place. Losing a job may rise deep fears or selfish gain to the surface that needs to be removed. The fall of a nation may happen to bring sin to the surface so there will be repentance to God. Uncertainties may raise anxiety to the surface so God can replace it with peace and the ability to trust Him. Finally, an illness can raise pain to the surface, so we'll depend on Him.

Let's know and remember, though, the difficult struggles we face are not caused by God, nor are they a form of punishment. As Paul tells us in Romans 3:23, everyone has sinned ever since Adam and Eve; we all fall short of God's glorious standards. Yet, God, in His grace, freely makes us right in His sight because of Jesus' sacrifice and redemption.

Therefore, the heat, or uncomfortable situations that cause us to meltdown, are not God's cruelty but become an opportunity for spiritual reformation, where He can make us pure and holy, with no more impurities. Whatever the challenge we face, God can turn it into something good. He can take challenging and even painful experiences and make them into something better than we would least expect. He is the Refiner, and we are gems or diamonds hidden in the rough that needs to be purified.

In the Bible, the prophet Zechariah tells us,

> "Awake, O sword, against my shepherd, against the man who stands next to me," declares the Lord of hosts.
>
> 'Strike the shepherd, and the sheep will be scattered; I will turn my hand against the little ones. In the whole land, declares the Lord, two thirds shall be cut off and perish, and one-third shall be left alive. And I will put this third into the fire, and

refine them as one refines silver, and test them as gold is tested. They will call upon my name, and I will answer them. I will say, 'They are my people; and they will say, 'The Lord is my God.'''

† Zechariah 13:7-9 (ESV)

Zechariah was a priest, and little did he know, he would also become a prophet. Being released from exile after 70 years of imprisonment in Babylon, he and his Jewish family were released when he was at a young age in his life.[2] After he became a priest, the Lord spoke to him about the coming of Messiah, and he proclaimed to the people in his town what the Lord told him. In the verse above, Zechariah told the people that God's shepherd was coming and how he would be stricken, and the sheep would scatter. In other words, Jesus, the Good Shepherd—God-made-man, is coming here, will be sacrificed to death, and when that happens, his sheep—or disciples, will scatter to different nations to spread the Gospel.

The Lord also told Zechariah that two-thirds of the people would perish, and one-third would be God's remnant whom He will refine. You see, Jesus lived through struggles and suffering, and as followers of Jesus, we're not promised a pain-free life with no struggles or meltdowns. Like Jesus, we'll experience trials and suffering. But because Jesus freely offered himself as our ultimate sacrifice for our sins and impurities, we'll experience praise, joy, and glory when the refining is finally complete, and we will look in the mirror at ourselves and see Jesus, too.

So how do we survive through this intense discomfort? How do we persevere through the suffering? From my own experience in the furnace, I learned that we must abide in the hope of Jesus' redemption. To abide means to entirely rely on God with every-thing in your life. To grow into deeper fellowship with the Lord, we must allow these spiritual meltdowns to teach us to surrender,

---

2   Chuck Swindoll. "Zechariah." *The Bible Teaching Ministry of Chuck Swindoll*, 2021, https://www.insight.org/resources/bible/the-minor-prophets/zechariah

to grow in endurance, patience, and hope. Unfortunately, it takes practice, but God must transform us into someone new.

In his book *No Man is an Island*, Thomas Merton warns us that our "society whose whole idea is to eliminate suffering and bring all its members the greatest amount of comfort and pleasure is doomed for destruction. It does not understand that all evil is not necessarily to be avoided."[3] Refinement is not necessarily evil, even though it can feel like it is sometimes. But isn't it true that we try our hardest to wipe out all pain and suffering because it is uncomfortable and unwanted? While living through a refining process or struggling, God allows our lives to boil up to remove our impurities for our good and His glory.

Refinement is not a quick process. We wonder if we'll ever feel relief. But when we are in the thick of being melted into liquid–like gold or silver, trapped in the furnace for days, weeks, months, or even years, we're in a moldable form. We are becoming purified each day into the beautiful image of Christ.

God is molding us as he is re-forming us into His image. As He is in the re-forming process, we must surrender ourselves and allow Him to do what He's good at doing—making us love more, live fuller, and reflect His Son, Jesus. We must trust and have hope in the Lord. He does this because of His compassion and love for us. He knows the best for us, and we must trust Him. It is not easy. It takes time. It can be uncomfortable. God's purpose of refinement is good. Be encouraged knowing that in the end, we are purified, made new, experience more profound joy, and it is more than worth it.

---

3   Thomas Merton. *No Man is an Island*, (Boston: Shambhala, 2005), p. 86–87

Personal Reflections

Do you feel like you're in the process of being refined by God today? Our hearts need to become melted down and pliable so God can shape us into His image. How do you see God reforming or reshaping you? What do you think your next step of refinement includes?

Isaiah 43:2–3, says "When you walk through the fire, you will not be burned; the flames will not set you ablaze. For I am the Lord your God, the Holy One of Israel, your Savior."

While in a season of refinement, does this promise from God encourage you? Does it strengthen you when you're in the process of being reformed? How?

Additional Scripture: Hebrews 12:1–13, Malachi 3:3, Isaiah 48:10

Personal Expressions

Author, Kris Camealy, gives a beautiful insight into refinement in her book, *Holey, Wholly and Holy: A Lenten Journey of Refinement*

"This is not a time to turn and run, though that may be our instinct. This is the time to stand still, to listen to what He's whispering, and to allow Him to strip you of the covers you've been hiding under. Trust me when I say you've not got anything He hasn't seen before. Stand in this fire, let Him purify you—this is how He loves us."[4]

4   Kris Camealy. *Holey, Wholly, Holy: A Lenten Journey of Refinement*, (2012) p. 18

Create a piece of art about the image that comes to your mind when you read it. Use whatever materials you choose. A suggestion might be to get hold of some clay or play dough and massage it to make it pliable so you can form it into something beautiful. Take your time, and as you mold the play dough, pray, thanking God for refining you to make you more like Himself.

🔊 **Listen to** *Refiner's Fire* **by Brian Doerksen**

Closing Prayer

Father, Son, and Holy Spirit, You existed before anything was created and is supreme over all creation. You said, "Let us make human beings in our image, to be like us." So, You created each of us in Your image, male and female. I confess my sins and know You forgive the sins of all who repent. You have tested me, O God; You have purified me like silver. Even though it isn't easy to be refined and re-formed, help me to trust You, my Refiner. Amen.

† (Colossians 1:15, Genesis 1:26–27, Psalm 38:18, Luke 24:27, Psalm 66:10)

CHAPTER 4

I'm Anxious

Opening Prayer

Almighty and merciful God, we lift up our hearts to thee for all who are the prey of anxious fears, who cannot get their minds off themselves, and to whom every demand brings the feeling that they cannot cope with what is required of them. Give them the comfort of knowing that this is illness, not cowardice; those millions have felt as they feel; that there is a way through this dark valley, a light at the end of it. Lead them to those who can show them the pathway to health and happiness. Sustain them by the knowledge that the Savior knows and understands all our woe and fear; and give them enough courage to face each day, and to rest their minds in the thought that thou wilt see the through.

† Leslie Weatherhead *In The House of Prayer*[1]

Those who live in the shelter of the Most High
  will find rest in the shadow of the Almighty.
This I declare about the Lord:
He alone is my refuge, my place of safety;
  he is my God, and I trust him.
For he will rescue you from every trap
  and protect you from deadly disease.
He will cover you with his feathers.

---

1   Leslie Weatherhead. *"The House of Prayer 1883-1975."* in *Between Heaven and Earth by Ken Giles,* (San Francisco, Harper Publishing, 1st edition February: 1997) p.104

He will shelter you with his wings.
His faithful promises are your armor and protection.
Do not be afraid of the terrors of the night,
  nor the arrow that flies in the day.
Do not dread the disease that stalks in darkness,
  nor the disaster that strikes at midday.
Though a thousand fall at your side,
  though ten thousand are dying around you,
  these evils will not touch you.
Just open your eyes,
  and see how the wicked are punished.

If you make the Lord your refuge,
  if you make the Most High your shelter,
  no evil will conquer you;
  no plague will come near your home.
For he will order his angels
  to protect you wherever you go.
They will hold you up with their hands
  so you won't even hurt your foot on a stone.
You will trample upon lions and cobras;
  you will crush fierce lions and serpents under your feet!

The Lord says, "I will rescue those who love me.
I will protect those who trust in my name.
When they call on me, I will answer;
I will be with them in trouble.
I will rescue and honor them.
I will reward them with a long life
  and give them my salvation."

† Psalm 91

Story

I was emptying the dishwasher after a long day at work, and to my husband's shock, I suddenly yelled, cursing the news anchor on the screen who was reporting about the increased political unrest in our country. I surprised myself, too, with the burst of ugly words. It came from built-up frustration, fear, and mental fatigue—the perfect formula to trigger an anxiety attack. Can you relate?

Raging, my heartbeat hard and heavy as I felt my face flush. My frustration and fear made me unexpectantly explode. Like every other person, I had tried to cope with the COVID-19 pandemic for months, virtual school and work, masks, riots, political unrest, holidays with broken traditions, and grief from loss. My fears were affecting me physically—the sudden onset of a panic attack exposed outward evidence of the state of my heart and mind.

Gratefully, the next day I was scheduled to go out of town for a personal, spiritual retreat to rest, pray and write this book. As I was praying, the Lord sweetly reminded me of the year 2012 when I'd had a similar attack of anxiety. How had I overcome it then?

I was reading Psalm 91 over and over again. I had printed it, taped it to my bathroom mirror, and read it every day.

Those who live in the shelter of the Most High will find rest in the shadows of the Almighty. This I declare about the Lord: He alone is my safety, my place of refuge; He is my God and I trust Him. For He will rescue you from every trap and protect you from deadly disease. He will cover you with his feathers. He will shelter you with his wings. His faithful promises are your armor and protection. (Psalm 91:1-4)

Psalm 91 was a melody that calmed my nerves. If anyone who walked on this earth understands how it feels to have an anxiety attack is Jesus. But Jesus? The Prince of Peace? The Light of the world?

The night before Jesus' crucifixion, his human emotions overtook him while he prayed in the Garden of Gethsemane. As part of the Trinity, He knew the pain and suffering he was about to endure, yet he experienced intense fear, depression, and anxiety because he was flesh like us.

While listening to an online women's conference, I heard the speaker describe the feelings and emotions Jesus experienced that night. Dr. Anita Phillips explained how Jesus was physically and mentally terrified, depressed, and anxious.

We read in Mark 14:32–34,

"They went to a place called Gethsemane, and Jesus said to his disciples, 'Sit here while I pray.' He took Peter, James, and John along with him, and he began to be deeply distressed and troubled. 'My soul is overwhelmed with sorrow to the point of death," he said to them. "Stay here and keep watch.'"

"Deeply distressed and troubled" give us only a glimpse of the intense emotions Jesus experienced. He had seen people hanging on crosses. He had witnessed people being beaten and flogged. He knew what he was about to experience. But more profoundly, he knew that he was about to experience sin for the first time. And not just one sin, but every sin of every person that was, is, and will be born. In preparation for his death, Jesus prayed.

"'Father, if you are willing, take this cup from me; yet not my will, but yours be done.' An angel from heaven appeared to him and strengthened him. And being in anguish, he prayed more earnestly, and his sweat was like drops of blood falling to the ground." (Luke 22:42–44).

What Jesus was experiencing is called "Hematohidrosis," a rare response to fear or stress, when capillaries, small blood vessels located around sweat glands, literally burst, causing someone to "sweat blood." This unusualness only occurs when someone is under extreme emotional or physical pressure.[2] While this is a rare condition, there are recorded incidences of this happening to people facing death, torture, or experiencing ongoing severe abuse.[3]

That night before his arrest, Jesus faced levels of fear, anxiety, and depression (Mark 14:32–42). Satan knew Jesus was weak and tried to take advantage of him. When we're in a situation where we feel anxious, we can also be prone to give in to temptation. When we are struggling, the enemy often dangles sin disguised as relief or help in front of our faces. He knows our faith can become fragile.

So how did Jesus get through those intense emotions?

He prayed. "Abba, Daddy, take this away from me." He was honest and asked, almost begged, God what he wanted. He wanted out of this situation. He wanted peace. Out of obedience to his Father, Jesus finished his prayer by saying—"but not my will, but Yours, Father." Somehow, someway, saying those words is an act of worship, and when we worship the Lord, He is exalted, and deep inside, we experience great joy in great suffering.

In his moments of desperation, Jesus relied on his knowledge of God's Word and went to it for strength. While fasting for forty days and nights, Satan tempted Jesus while he was weak and hungry, yet speaking God's ancient words gave Jesus the stamina he needed. Scripture doesn't tell us what Scripture he may have had on his mind while he prayed in the Garden of Gethsemane, but perhaps the Holy Spirit reminded him of David's Psalm 91: "For he will order his angels to protect you wherever you go." (91:11), and then God sent an angel to strengthen His Son. (Luke 22:43)

---

2 Dr. Anita Phillips. "The Emotional Highs and Lows of Leadership." *IF:Lead Online Conference* September 2020, www.ifgathering.com/iflead2020
3 Debra Jaliman, MD. on 3 February 2020, WebMD, accessed 7 March 2020, https://www.webmd.com/a-to-z-guides/hematidrosis-hematohidrosis#1-4

Another way Jesus was able to face the anxiety of His own death is because he trusted His Father. Jesus trusted in the Lord with all his heart, mind, and soul and didn't lean on his own understanding.[4] In all his ways, he acknowledged his Father; therefore, God made Jesus' path straight. Jesus trusted God to give him the strength he needed, and he trusted God through the next step, which was to surrender to the Romans who sought to arrest him. He trusted God enough to know that his Father still loved him, even though He did not remove the burden from him.

Jesus came to redeem us and save us from our sins, and his ultimate sacrifice also shows us that he understands what we're going through. Jesus knows what it's like for us to live in a corrupt and scary world that causes us to mentally and physically break down. He experienced it too.

We have an emotional connection with Jesus because he felt those primary and raw feelings, too.[5] We may still have to battle sickness, abuse, loss, loneliness, and more. We may be trying to single-parent disobedient kids, be going through a divorce, or have all normalcy quickly ripped away from us through any number of adversities. We are not freed from those struggles, just as Jesus wasn't. But because of Jesus' own suffering, we can have hope that there are better days to come. Jesus had to believe there were better days to come with His Father, and so do we. Until those days come, let's hold onto the truth that Jesus understands us, is there for us, and provides us with what we need.

"When they call on Me, I will answer;
I will be with them in trouble.
I will rescue and honor them.
I will reward them with a long life
and give them my salvation." † **Psalm 91:15–16**

---

4   Proverbs 3:5–6 paraphrased
5   Dr. Anita Phillips. "The Emotional Highs and Lows of Leadership." *IF:Lead Online Conference* September 2020, www.ifgathering.com/iflead2020

Personal Reflections

If you're able, think about those things which make you feel anxious. What can you do to limit your exposure to these triggers? If memories trigger emotional unrest, make a list of the promises God gives you in His Word; maybe begin with Psalm 91.

Go to a quiet place alone. Sit down. Be still. Then say this: "I'm OK. Even though I'm not OK and feel .... On a scale of 1–10, the intensity of this feeling is ...." Then you can go on and say this: "I am a human being. It's normal to feel .... Jesus felt this feeling too, and the Holy Spirit is praying for me as I walk through it." After saying that, close your eyes and begin scanning your body from your head to your toes. Where do you feel emotionally tense in your body? Negative emotions can cause your jaws to tighten, shoulders to hunch, stomach to churn, or your chest feels tight. Stop there. Take a deep breath in and release that tension as you exhale. Imagine seeing that tension leave your body as God's angel strengthens you like he did Jesus. Continue to take deep breaths and exhale those tensions. Do that through-out your entire body as you let everything go.

(I learned this practice from Dr. Anita Phillips, a well-known trauma therapist who weaves together mental health, faith, and culture.)

Additional Scripture: Matthew 6:25–26, Philippians 4:6–9, Daniel 7:15, 8:27

Personal Expressions

Read Philippians 4:8. Do what it says and think about such things. Practice trading anxious, fearful thoughts for thoughts about things that are good, true, and lovely. Then, if you're able, print a small copy of a picture of Auguste Rodin's sculpture called "The Thinker" or draw one. Then, somewhere on that paper, write the words NOBLE, RIGHT, PURE, LOVELY, ADMIRABLE, EXCELLENT, and PRAISEWORTHY. Put it in a place that you will frequently see and think about things that make you feel like those words.[6]

🔊 **Listen to** *My Hallelujah* **by Bryan and Katie Torwalt**

Closing Prayer

LORD, I choose to trust You with all my heart and not depend on my own understanding. I want to seek Your will in all I do. God, You are my Wonderful Counselor. You have searched me, and you know me. Before a word is on my tongue, You know it completely, Oh Lord. Where can I go from Your Spirit? Please help me remember that Your Son, Jesus, knows how I feel and reminds me that I am not alone when negative emotions arise. Help me replace my feelings of fear and anxiety with peace and hope. Amen.

† (Proverbs 3:5-6, Isaiah 9:6, Psalm 139:4)

*If you are experiencing anxiety or panic attacks, consult your medical doctor or schedule an appointment with a psychiatrist. It's OK to do that. It's good to do that.

---

6   This is a lesson taught by Jane Albright, former NCAA Women's Basketball coach at a Fellowship of Christian Athletes meeting in October 2019 at Elon University.

CHAPTER 5

Opening Prayer

My Father, Closer to me than my own heartbeat...more urgent to my life than the air I'm breathing...thank you, Father, that you allow nothing to keep us apart today!"

† **Amy Carmichael: *I Come Quietly to Meet You*[1]**

I am convinced that nothing can ever separate us from God's love. Neither death nor life, neither angels nor demons, neither our fears for today nor our worries about tomorrow—not even the powers of hell can separate us from God's love. No power in the sky above or in the earth below—indeed, nothing in all creation will ever be able to separate us from the love of God that is revealed in Christ Jesus our Lord. † **Romans 8:38-39**

Story

After getting my kids off to school, I go to my part-time job, where I share an office with a friend. Across the narrow hall is another office with two other women, and we chatted off and on during the morning. After clocking out of work, I drive to a

---

1 *Amy Carmichael: I Come Quietly to Meet You,* (Minneapolis, Minnesota, Bethany House Publishers, 2005) p. 82

local restaurant to meet a friend for a late lunch, where we catch each other up on our busy lives. On the way home, stopping at the grocery store to pick up a few things, I bump into the mom of my daughter's friend in the produce section, and we chat. As I pull into the driveway, the kids pull in right behind me, coming home from school. We share how our days have been, I scroll through social media photos and comments, then begin cooking dinner. My husband comes home from work, we sit down as a family to eat, and then I rush out the door to go to a meeting. Once home, I listen to the 10 pm news while at the same time scrolling through my emails, play some Wordscape games on my phone, and then call it a day.

Hardly ever was there a time that day, and most days, when I was alone, except when driving to and from work. So why did I often feel both hollow and somehow heavy at the same time? Why did I live daily with a gut feeling of loneliness when I was blessed with a loving family, had more friends than I deserve, and held leadership roles at church ministries and community groups?

I kept this inner conflict a secret. I made sure the outside of me was doing life the way many do life these days. I stayed busy. I have a family, a job, errands to run, and other activities that we take pictures of and post on social media so that our lives look happy and perfect. However, the inside of me was the opposite of what I portrayed.

When taking most personality tests, I've learned that half of me is an extrovert while half is an introvert. Ironically, I've craved and carved out time to be alone most of my life, but something different was taking place in my daily, recharging minutes of sweet solitude. The desired and needful alone-time, which included time with Jesus, became a lonesome-time. The feeling I was experiencing was one I had never expected, much less understood. This loneliness had slowly evolved through several months, unknowingly, making itself warm and cozy in my soul, discretely suffocating companionship with Jesus that used to fill that space.

For over 20 years, fellowship with God had evolved into a beautiful tapestry of prayer, life-giving Truth, little yet undoubtedly revelations of His presence, power, hope, and love. But after several months, it felt as if all those moments were snatched away from me—with no more in sight ahead, either.

Then, one day I noticed. I more than noticed. It felt as if I woke up one morning, doing my everyday things, went to meet with God to start the day, and realized I was utterly, almost eerily, alone. Where was He? I thought back to what I may have done to cause Him not to show up, and I remember that over the past few months, our conversations had become shorter because I was allowing distractions and worry to interrupt that time with Him. That time which had been so life-giving, now felt lifeless. The more I thought about it, it *did* feel like I had been talking to a brick wall. The prayer requests I had been asking, even pleading with God, day after day, to relieve me from struggles, kept bouncing back to me. Only silence. A painful silence, and a feeling of abandonment, as if God had left me alone for my starving soul to fend for itself.

That's when and where loneliness found a new home in that empty space. Do you ever feel that way?

Thankfully, by the grace of God, He revealed to me, in His perfect timing (even though it didn't feel perfect to me), that Jesus truly *did* know how I felt. And he knows how you feel, too.

To begin with, we don't have to be alone to experience loneliness. I kept a full schedule to stay busy to avoid feeling lonely, but that did not work. Jesus experienced loneliness firsthand. Jesus was flesh and blood. He felt lonely as a child and teenager because even though he played and did chores, he was slightly different from his siblings and peers. No one seemed to be as close to God as he was.

Jesus developed deep friendships with his disciples over the three years of his ministry with them by his side. In the back of his mind, though, he had a mission to accomplish that no one else could do, and no one could understand the weight of his responsibilities.

Jesus was led into the desert to be tempted by Satan for forty days. There was no one to encourage him, bring him food to eat, or water to drink. There was no one with him to keep him company, hold him accountable, or pray with him.

And remember, Jesus was abandoned in the Garden of Gethsemane when his closest friends fell asleep after he had asked them to stand guard and pray for him, in the deepest and darkest hour of his life to that point.

And then, Jesus felt alone and abandoned as he suffered on the cross until his death; He was separated from his Father, God.

There are different levels of loneliness. There's the kind where you've been out of town by yourself for work, and you miss your family and routines. There's loneliness when someone close to you dies. There's loneliness when no one seems to understand how you feel because you're the only one you know who has experienced the hurt you have. But there is one kind of loneliness that cuts deeper than any other. That is the loneliness when it feels like Abba, your Father, isn't near you. You've cried out to Him to take away your grief, pain, and turmoil. You've pleaded to feel His presence, not only in your heart but even deeper in your soul. But nothing. Silence. Isolation. Separation.

I think it's kind of an oxymoron how Jesus felt lonely even though he had an intimate relationship with his Father. But think about that. Have you ever felt that way too? I know I have. So how did Jesus cope with loneliness? Jesus intentionally went to God in prayer because that kept him going through the human struggles and emotions he faced. Jesus knew it was essential to have time alone with God to prepare him for the days ahead and because he wanted to stay connected with Someone who listened to him and gave him wisdom and love in return. Even at the beginning of God's Story, in Genesis 2:18, it is written that man is not to be alone. God created us to be in communion with others. Even God is not alone because He is part of the Trinity. God created us to need a friend, to have a village of people in our lives to bless and be blessed. From our own seasons of struggling, we know that it's not healthy to be alone for an extended time. I know from experience that seeking community when you're struggling is easier said than done, but intentionally isolating yourself is unhealthy.

Never forget that Jesus understands you when you feel lonely. His Spirit is present with you even if you're in a crowded room or your car alone. So cry out to Jesus for companionship, and if you don't feel it immediately, keep crying out. The loneliness Jesus felt didn't last forever. It was temporary. And that is a promise for you and me, too.

Paul told the Corinthians, and us, this promise:

> *"For our present troubles are small and won't last very long. Yet they produce for us a glory that vastly outweighs them and will last forever!"* † **(2 Cor. 4:17)**

Jesus also promises us that when we come to him, with whatever struggle or sin tying us down, he will never cast us out or away from himself.[2] You never need to feel lonely because he says, "Come to me, says Christ. I will embrace you into my deepest being and never let you go."[3] May you know that you are not alone, even if you feel lonely. May you know you are heard, even if you feel like you're talking to yourself. May you know you are connected to the Source that gives communion, Who understands you and will always be with you.

---

2   John 6:37
3   Dane Ortlund. *Gentle and Lowly: The Heart of Christ for Sinners and Sufferers,* (Wheaton, Illinois: Crossway, 2020) p. 66

Personal Reflections

Describe a time in your life when you struggled with prolonged loneliness. What triggered this struggle? What made it worse? What makes it better?

Do you feel comfortable admitting to other people in your life when you feel lonely? Why or why not? Read Psalm 25:16–21 about David's lament. Why do you think he was willing, to be honest in this struggle?

Additional Scripture: Ecclesiastes 4:9–12, Matthew 28:18–20, John 16:31–33

Personal Expressions

Research has shown that participating in different forms of creative arts helps a person's overall health when struggling with loneliness. Some doctors might begin prescribing music and visual arts alongside or instead of medication.[4] If you have a local theater, orchestra, singing group, or art gallery in your community, invite a family member, friend, or co-worker to attend it with you. Enjoy the atmosphere, enjoy the company, listen, and observe. Invite the Holy Spirit to be present with you at your activity or event, too!

🔊 **Listen to *I Will Carry You* by Ellie Holcomb**

---

4   Jon Bloom. "Jesus Understands Your Loneliness." *Desiring God,* 27 July 2018, https://www.desiringgod.org/articles/jesus-understands-your-loneliness

Closing Prayer

Who will not fear you, Lord, and glorify Your name? For You alone are holy. All nations will come and worship before You, for Your righteous deeds have been revealed. Lord, hear my prayer! Listen to my plea! Don't turn away from me in my time of distress. Bend down to listen and answer me quickly when I call to You. For my days disappear like smoke, and my bones burn like red-hot coals. My heart is sick. I lie awake, lonely as a solitary bird on the roof. Yet, I trust You are with me. Let Your unfailing love surround me, Lord, for my hope is in You alone. Amen.

† (Revelations 15:4, Psalm 102:1-4 and 7, Psalm 33:2)

PART TWO

Hues of
Gray

CHAPTER 6

Hiding

Opening Prayer

It is you, O hidden One, who has given me my heritage, and you determined the place of my birth. It is you who have given me the power to do one kind or work and withheld the skill to do another. It is you who hold in your hand the threads of this day's life and you alone who know what lies before me to do or to suffer. But because you are my Father, I am not afraid. Because it is your Spirit that stirs within my heart's most special room, I know that all is well.

† John Baillie A Diary of Private Prayer[1]

For you died to this life, and your real life is hidden with Christ in God. And when Christ, who is your life, is revealed to the whole world, you will share in all his glory. † **Colossians 3:3-4**

Story

Ms. Ara Tizi was an older woman with coarse, black hair scattered with streaks of silver. She had unique characteristics that matched her unusual name. One of the things I remember most about her was her loud voice, which she needed because she loved working

---

1   John Baillie. A Diary of Private Prayer: A Devotional Classic, updated and revised by Susanna Wright (New York: Scribner, A Division of Simon & Schuster, Inc 1949) p. 35

with kids, loved encouraging us to get our hands messy, and loved to direct puppet shows about stories from the Bible.

When I was about ten years old, I excitedly woke up many Saturday mornings because my dad drove me to church. I enjoyed that time because I could use my imagination and be messy with other kids. Ms. Tizi created and directed a vibrant "Puppet Ministry." Some of my favorite childhood memories include those few years I made puppets, rehearsed for our performances, and put on shows for our parents to enjoy. Very unprofessional? Yes. Very entertaining? Yes!

It was a process. First, we needed to make the puppets. The tables held balloons, strips of newspaper, and big bowls of goopy substance. After blowing up our balloons, we dipped the newspaper strips into the bowl of watered-down glue, then smoothed the strips around the air-tight balloon. Oh, the joy-filled feeling of sticky fingers as I formed my puppet's forehead, eye sockets, nose, and chin. While the head dried, we moved to the next station, to a table covered with colorful scraps of fabric we could choose from to become our puppets' clothes.

The following Saturday involved painting our puppets' faces and gluing yarn on the head to give them hair. The fabric for their clothing adhered to the puppets' necks. To finish them, Ms. Tizi had collected tiny hats, crowns, shepherd hooks, and other props to help our puppets come alive.

Someone from our church built a wooden puppet stage, and Ms. Tizi made two purple curtains to make the mini-theater look real. For a few weeks, we rehearsed our lines of the Bible story we were performing on our knees. We worked especially hard at keeping our puppets up high, not lowering them while we read our lines. It was a tight squeeze when four or five of us crawled behind the stage with our puppets.

From those memories, the two things I loved most were creating the puppets and hiding behind the curtain. No one in the audience saw me behind the stage. I couldn't trip in front of the audience, and

I didn't have to worry about forgetting my lines because I could read them from the script if needed. As an adult now, I see when the comfort of hiding began—first during puppet shows, then in my real life, too.

I didn't realize I was hiding then, but looking back to when I was a child, I recall how not only did I hide behind a puppet stage but also under my covers in my bed. For several months I feared our house would catch on fire in the middle of the night. The loud firework booms on the fourth of July sent me crawling under the car seats, trembling, while the bright display of colors danced in the hot, summer night sky.

The word *hide* can have more than one meaning. There's a difference between hiding *from* someone or something and hiding *in* someone or something.

There can be the skill of hiding, and there can be the art of hiding.

When thinking of the meaning of *hiding from*, we tend to think of skillfully figuring out how not to be seen or revealed. When something is hidden from, it's being kept from others so as not to be discovered. Something *hidden from* is intentionally in the shadows of darkness and makes one feel invisible, covered, and avoided.

I became an expert hider.

As I grew out of my childhood fears, teenage worries replaced them—approval from others and people-pleasing. One of my number one missions was to be a good girl in the eyes of others. I didn't want anyone to be upset with me, and I didn't want to be a burden in anyone's life. I wanted everyone to like me and would conform to please others. Today, people say I'm a good listener. That's because I had much practice in those formative years when several friends confided in me all their gossip and worries. I just listened, uh-huh'ed, nodded, or shook my head, and kept asking questions until we ran out of time because I didn't want there to be time for me to talk.

As I grew up, got married, had children, and learned to do all the adulting things adults do, my hiding didn't go away. Still wanting approval from others and not sharing my personal feelings on many things, including my faith, became my way of living. *It became a bad habit,* and I got pretty good at it. Even after I had given my life to Jesus in college, I continued to hide behind the "good girl" mask while on the inside, I struggled with my identity in Christ, depression, and doubt about the fact that I am God's beloved in whom Christ dwells and delights.

The past few years, as I've been learning the art of struggling, Jesus has been showing me in His Word a different kind of hiding. But, before we look into that, let's remember how Jesus didn't hide. He didn't hide from his enemies, the Pharisees, he didn't hide his true self to get the approval of the fishermen, so they'd follow him or the people in the towns he visited. In his flesh, Jesus was concerned the religious leaders were plotting to kill him, but it did not stop him from doing what the Lord called him to do. And he didn't give in to the peer pressure or rules to conform to lifeless, religious rituals.

Most of all, Jesus did not hide from death on the cross. Jesus did not hide his obedience to God, gentleness towards others, or mission to expand God's Kingdom.

Some of us are doing our own "hiding from." Maybe it's the kind where we're scrolling through social media reading the harsh opinions about a topic that makes it feel hard to breathe but still won't let anyone know about our anxiety. Or it's the kind of hiding where we don't tell our family or our close friend that we cry more than usual. Or the kind where a past sin that we have redeemed from years ago still weighs on us, but we don't dare tell anyone else—these kinds of hiding work against us.

Having learned the hard way, I now know that it's not healthy to hide your struggles and withhold your negative emotions. Feeling sad, fearful, anxious, or depressed happens to all of us in life. However, when those negative feelings are kept secret from others, especially for an extended time, we risk jeopardizing relationships, weakening our physical bodies, and causing harm to our mental health.

Not only do we hide from others, but we also try to hide from God, just like Adam and Eve did when they hid behind bushes after they sinned. David even told us, when he wrote Psalm 139, "Lord, you know everything there is to know about me. You perceive every movement of my heart and soul, and you understand my every thought before it even enters my mind."[2]

To those who have chronic hiding habits, I have good news! There is a safe and healthy place we *can* hide. That place is *in Christ.*

Paul's letter to the Colossians and us states, "For you died to this life, and your real life is hidden with Christ in God."

Do you remember the descriptions of the meaning of *hiding from*? Well, here are the descriptions of the meaning of *hiding in. Hiding in* means we can think of something not *yet* revealed. When something is hidden in, it's being protected for safekeeping. However, being *hidden in* also stirs anticipation for something to be discovered, uncovered, and brought to the light.

So, how can we hide in an invisible God? When we proclaim that Jesus is our Savior, that he redeems us from our sins, invites us to baptism, and communion with him at his Table, we receive a new life. To be given a new life means our old life has died.

Jesus gave us an example of one way we can hide in God. Woven through the four gospels, Jesus intentionally hid away regularly, in a cave or the woods, to rest his body, commune with his Father, and get re-energized to continue his calling and purpose.

As Paul tells us, our new life is hidden with Christ in God. It is hidden because God promised us eternal life with His Trinity on

2 Psalm 139:1-2 (The Passion Translation)

the new earth, in heaven, and we cannot see that yet. But doesn't that rouse sweet anticipation of what is yet to come? Until the day we reach heaven, God protects us, defends us, and as David described, God shields us and is our place of safety (Psalm 18:2). God hides you, the unique and beautiful you, within Himself. While you're in His special hiding place, He's also repairing your brokenness and strengthening your faith so you can stop *hiding from* the things and people in your life who need you.

Personal Reflections

Today, do you find yourself *hiding from* God or *hiding in* God? Why? How are you doing that? If you're hiding from God, why do you think it can be challenging to be vulnerable to Him?

In what 'earthly' ways do you try to find safety, security, and significance?

Additional Scripture: Psalm 32:7, Psalm 119:114, Psalm 17:8, Psalm 27:5, Genesis 3

Personal Expressions

Below are some of the lyrics to the hymn *Rock of Ages* from Augustus Montague Toplady (1740-1778). With paper, markers, paint, play dough, whatever you have to access, create a depiction of what comes to your mind and heart when reading these lines about hiding yourself in God?

Rock of Ages, cleft for me,
Let me hide myself in Thee;
Let the water and the blood,
From Thy riven side which flowed

Closing Prayer

Lord, You hide me in the shelter of Your presence, safe from those who conspire against me. In You, I am safe from accusing tongues. Let me live forever in Your sanctuary, safe beneath the shelter of Your wings! You are my secret, secure, safe, and comfortable hiding place. You are the perfect example of how I should and should not hide. Thank You for still loving me when I've chosen to hide from You instead of hiding in You. Thank You for the gift to be able to hide in You with the sweet anticipation of heaven. Amen.

† (Psalm 31:20, Psalm 61:4)

CHAPTER 7

Doubting God

Opening Prayer

Father, I abandon myself into your hands; do with me what you will. Whatever you may do, I thank you: I am ready for all, I accept all. Let only your will be done in me, and in all your creatures—I wish no more than this, O Lord.

† Richard J. Foster *Prayer: Finding the Heart's True Home*[1]

This is my command—be strong and courageous! Do not be afraid or discouraged. For the Lord, your God is with you wherever you go."

† Joshua 1:9

Story

He was a plain farmer and an outcast in the lowest class in society. Luckily, he had a job threshing wheat, even though it paid very little. He rose with the sun and worked in a field as hidden as possible so the upper- and middle-class people nearby would not see him. If they did, they would physically and verbally hurt him just because they didn't think he was worthy of anything.

---

1 As quoted in Roger Pooley and Philip Seddon, eds. and comps., *The Lord of the Journey: A Reader in Christian Spirituality* (San Francisco: Collins Liturgical in USA, 1986) p. 292

Little did he know that this day would be different from all the ordinary days, a day he never imagined and one he would not soon forget. Late morning, he stopped to rest a moment to give his arms, shoulders, and back a break from threshing. Up and down. Up and down, beating the light brown chaffs of wheat on a large, flat rock. Walking over to get some shade under a knotted oak tree, startled, he jerked back because he saw another man sitting where he planned to sit. The farmer did not recall ever seeing this unusual and captivating person before.

To the farmer's surprise again, this strange visitor said, "The Lord is with you, mighty warrior."

"*Me*, a mighty warrior? I don't think so," the farmer said with a laugh. "The Lord, who supposedly is called a miracle-worker, didn't rescue us from the Midian's who treat us horribly. My grandparents used to tell me how God saved and delivered them from Egypt into the Promised Land. Well, he isn't delivering us from turmoil and leading us to a better place. Instead, the Lord abandoned us."

The farmer did not expect this visitor's reply to be, "Go in the strength you have and save your people from your enemies." But it was.

"Seriously?" the farmer thought.

Gideon's journey started when he was a farmer in the book of Judges. The Visitor was God. Let's take a deeper dive into the heart and mind of Gideon because if you're like me, you've more than likely felt like he did at some point in your life.

For many years, Gideon's meager job was threshing wheat. Since I didn't grow up on a farm, I wasn't familiar with the process. I learned that threshing is when the grain separates from its stalk or chaff by beating it against another surface. These days, at least in America, farmers use high-tech equipment and efficient machines to get as much of the brunt work accomplished.

But throughout most of history, including around 1220 BC, farmers manually did the job by hand. They held a bundle of chaffs of wheat and beat them on a hard, flat surface like a rock to release the grain from the chaff. In more recent history, a farmer lowered the bundle of chafes into an empty container, like a trash can, and vigorously beat the chaffs back and forth. By doing this, the grain of wheat falls to the bottom of the container. It was a laborious job.

Gideon had been beating chaffs of wheat against a rock day after day for a long time. With that repetition out in the field, he had time to think. It's clear from the reading that Gideon struggled with doubt and lacked confidence in God. Gideon—a mighty warrior? He struggled to obey God's commands to be strong and courageous because he lacked confidence. Gideon's forefathers had been confident when Moses saved them from slavery and led them through the desert to the Promised Land, so he should, too. Instead, as he beat the chaffs of wheat all day, he beat himself up with negative words like an incompetent, weakest of the weak, nobody who doubted God's compassion for him and clan. So, when God (the Visitor) showed up telling Gideon he's a mighty warrior, he thought this stranger was joking around with him. Although, Gideon probably didn't think it was amusing.

"Pardon me, but the Lord who says He's with us abandoned us, so the Midians overtook us. The Lord was with Moses and my forefathers, but no, He's not been with us." Gideon said that with sarcasm in his voice because he doubted the Lord.

"Go in the strength you have and save Israel," God responded.

Gideon repeatedly questioned God, which caused him to doubt his own self. Where had his confidence in the Lord gone? Had it dried up like wheat? He felt puny, numb, and defeated and told himself those lies self-consciously each day. The lie he accepted said that he was inadequate and unqualified to do anything other than thresh wheat in a winepress. Does that sound familiar to you?

God, You think I can lead a war? I think I'd be better at threshing wheat.

God, I must have misunderstood You when You nudged me to lead a new Bible Study. But, unfortunately, only three people signed up to attend, probably because they think I'm an inadequate teacher, so maybe I'll cancel it.

God, how can You truly forgive me of the sins I've committed?

God, I've been praying and asking You for months to take me out of this valley, but You haven't. Do you love me anymore?

God, every time I talk to my parents about my faith, they change the subject or get upset with me. So what's the point of continuing to try?

God, I believe in You and try to live a life pleasing to You, so why are You allowing me to suffer?

If you've been a Christ-follower, you've gone through a stage, or stages, of growth in your faith. The Word has come alive to you, your pastor's ministry to you, and listening to worship music in the car as you run errands is a holy experience. I'm grateful many of my days in my life have felt that way, yet there have been other days when I've felt the opposite—lifeless, cloudy, and gray. When those days pile on top of each other, along with unanswered prayers, doubts begin to form. Doubts that God is ignoring me, turning His back against me, and is more concerned about other people than myself. Have you ever worried that God has abandoned you because you keep intentionally sinning? Have you felt separated from Him because you've prayed and read the Bible and asked to feel His presence but felt nothing? Have you doubted that you are God's beloved and felt tempted to give up your faith in Him? If you said yes to any of those questions, then you're not alone. But, unfortunately, those doubts run deep, and due to that feeling, we've threshed ourselves by beating ourselves with inaccurate descriptions like a failure, loser, or unworthy.

When I was at that point once in my life, thinking that maybe God was in a chaffing mood again, picking on *me* instead of Gideon this time, God's Spirit brought this question to my mind,

"Have you ever thought that the way you beat yourself with negative self-talk insults Me because I created you?" I thought about how God made me in His image and how these negative doubts against myself hurt us both. I didn't want to hurt Him! His tone was gentle, tender, and loving, and I knew He was right. But, I also knew I was at the point where I needed to surrender my doubts about myself and Him.

Isn't it interesting how the opposite of the word *thresh* is *still* or *surrender*? God asked Gideon to surrender his self-doubt to the Mighty Warrior when it came down to the nitty-gritty. He wanted Gideon to surrender his low self-esteem, the illness of believing the lies the enemy was telling him, and was asking Gideon to stop beating himself up with harsh words.

To experience the joy and purpose God has for you, surrendering your doubts to the Lord is essential. Here's an alert, though. It is not effortless, and it is an uncomfortable, ongoing process that will finally come to completion when we take our last breath on this earth. Surrender takes place when we give our whole selves to Him, not just part of ourselves. It is a process because it takes time; we usually prefer to hold onto comfort and control instead of embracing difficulty and sacrifice. Surrender can also be painful because it can feel like being threshed, yet it's the start of something completely new. To be used, the wheat must be threshed and the chaff removed. God promises that He will be with us through the chaffing and will celebrate with us in the harvest.

Through words, author Kris Camealy paints a collage of soul-provoking questions about surrender in her book *Everything Is Yours.*

"What if, instead of shaking our fists and demanding an explanation, we looked for what God does in our suffering? What if, rather than chasing that ever-elusive 'why?' we turned our energy towards learning new ways of faithfulness in difficulty? What if we saw the trouble of our lives as an invitation to a more intentional, intimate relationship with our God? What if, in the midst of our heartbreak, we actually invited God more fully into our pain rather than rejecting Him because of it?"[2]

To stop doubting ourselves and God, we must surrender ourselves to God. When we surrender our doubts, our worries, our sin, even our spiritual desires, to God, it is then when we experience confidence through Christ. The writer of the book of Hebrews declared this truth: "*So do not throw away this confident trust in the Lord. Remember the great reward it brings you!*" (Hebrews 10:35)

That is what Gideon's Visitor, the Lord, wanted. He wanted Gideon to confidently trust Him, which is the opposite of doubting Him. When you continue to read the chapters after Judges 6, you'll learn that by Gideon doing so, the Visitor would reward him by making him a mighty warrior to win battles against his enemy. The record shows us how God commands us to trust Him throughout the Bible. May we choose to trust instead of doubt. May we choose to worship instead of insult God. May we surrender ourselves to God instead of giving in to the Enemy's attack. May we be God's equipped and mighty warriors ready to fight a battle against any doubt that charges forward.

---

2 Kris Camealy. *Everything Is Yours: How Giving God Your Whole Heart Changes Your Whole Life*, (Westerville, OH: Refine Media, 2019) p.100

Personal Reflections

What is your reaction when you hear the word "surrender"? Then, write your definition of surrender.

Spiritually, do you feel like you're in a stage of growth, chaffing, or harvest? Do you feel like you're growing closer to God and reaching closer to the Son? Or do you feel chaffed—having been separated from your root of faith? Or do you feel you're in a harvest season reaping the blessings and provisions He has given you in your life? Explore which one you think you're in and why.

Additional Scripture: Judges 6: 11–22, Luke 24:36–43, James 1:2–8

Personal Expressions

In your art journal, using the supplies of your choice, create a picture of the stage you're currently in—growth, chaffing, or harvest. Be creative! (I got this idea from Kris Camealy in her book *Everything Is Yours*, where she beautifully teaches how surrendering to God goes through phases as well.)

🔊 **Listen to** *Prove Me Wrong* **by Caedmon's Call**

Closing Prayer

Sovereign Lord, Who is mighty to save, You want me to surrender my all to You. I confess I have doubted Your goodness in my life. Forgive me for holding onto the things that keep me from truly surrendering my whole self to You. Please help me to relinquish my doubts. In your Word, You say time after time not to be afraid and do not doubt You. In quietness and confidence in You, You give me strength. I want and need to remember that truth. Thank You for Your Word, like a lamp shining in a dark place until the Day comes. When doubt fills my mind, Your comfort gives me renewed hope and cheer. Amen.

† (Psalm 106:8, Ezekiel 44:9, Joshua 1:9, Matthew 14:31, Isaiah 30:15 2 Peter 1:19, Psalm 94:19)

CHAPTER 8

Unwanted Thorns

Opening Prayer

Have worn my stumbling feet:
Oh, soothe me with thy smiles,
And make my life complete.
The thorns were thick and keen
Where 'er I trembling trod;
The way was long between

My O LORD, the hard-won miles
Wounded feed and God.
Where healing waters flow
Do thou my footsteps lead.
My heart is aching so;
Thy gracious balm I need.

† Paul Laurence Dubar "A Prayer"[1]

Then Pilate had Jesus flogged with a lead-tipped whip. The soldiers wove a crown of thorns and put it on his head, and they put a purple robe on him. "Hail! King of the Jews!" they mocked, as they slapped him across the face. **† John 19:1–3**

Story

Ouch!

I glared at my pointer finger for getting in the way of the thorn attached to the rose bush. In North Carolina, even though I'm not a fan of summer's hot humidity and daily mosquito bites, I

---

1 P.L. Dunbar. *The Complete Poems of Paul Laurence Dunbar,* (New York: Dodd, Mead, and Company, 1913)

still enjoy going into the yard to cut flowers to make a bouquet for the kitchen table. Roses are some of my favorite flowers. My entire life, I've observed my mom take good care of her rose bushes, and I'm grateful she has trained me along the way.

I have a few bushes of my own now that I've nurtured over the years. One sticky, summer evening I decided to tend to my rose bushes. I don't remember if I was in a hurry or too lazy to take the time to put on my gardening gloves, but I only grabbed the rose clippers in the garage on my way outside. While clipping half-eaten leaves off the bushes that aphids had munched on and pruning some brown, spotted leaves, I reached deeper into the rose bush with my bare hand.

"Ouch!"

Naturally, I yanked my hand towards myself and looked down to see a plump, deep red drop of blood blooming on my finger that stung with pain. So, I went back inside to wash the blood off my finger. This was not the first time getting pricked by a thorn, but I noticed something different when looking at my cleaned finger.

A new, unwelcome guest was wedged deep inside my finger—a thorn. For the next several minutes, I picked my finger several times with a pin and tweezers trying to get the thorn out of the most tender part of my pointer finger, but I was unsuccessful. I figured it would come out on its own in a few days and settled in for the evening.

Days became weeks, and weeks became months. That small, sharp thorn had found a new home deep in my finger. When rubbing over the small lump on the tip of my splintered finger, a dull pain triggered memories of the painful thorns in my life. Those thorns seemed to be stuck in my soul, too.

Thorns are part of life, aren't they? Not just the ones on rose stems, but ones that prick and pierce our heart and mind and wedge into our soul. Those "thorns" can be a discomfort, a constant bother, even painful. Thorns can be a lifetime battle with a chronic disease, a bitter experience from former years that still comes back to haunt you, or a family member that debates everything you say.

My "thorns" have been with me for almost 30 years. And it's not the tender-to-touch rose thorn in my finger. These longtime thorns pierced my life when a sharp blade cut through my head as doctors performed the surgery. God spared my life because I had a 50/50 chance of coming out alive after brain surgery. By my surgeon's skills, the tangle in my brain became untangled, but some other lifetime struggles appeared that I was not expecting: a loss of vision, trouble to find the words I want to say (called aphasia), and flares of chemical imbalance in my brain due to the trauma my brain experienced when it underwent surgery. Okay, I'll say the word—depression.

Those are the thorns deeply embedded into my body that probably will not come out in this lifetime. (The real rose thorn in my finger did eventually come out almost a year later.)

Thorns go back to the beginning in the third chapter of Genesis. They continually grow and weave themselves throughout God's story in the Bible and each of our lives today. In Genesis 3, Adam and Eve gave in to the serpent and ate the fruit from the Tree of Life that God had explicitly instructed them not to do. After they disobeyed, God told Satan, Adam, and Eve their consequences, including being cast out of the Garden, east of Eden. Satan will be crushed to death, and Adam and Eve will experience thorns and thistles, in other words, struggles.

In his book, *The Advent of the Lamb of God*, Russ Ramsey fittingly wrote, "When the dust in Eden settled, things were different. Coming into this world would be a struggle. Living in this world would be a struggle. Leaving this world would be a struggle," and that every one of us will "struggle from the cradle to the grave as the heirs to the first parents' sin."[2]

> *"Cursed is the ground because of you; through painful toil, you will eat of it all the days of your life. It will produce thorns and thistles for you, and you will eat the plants of the field."*
>
> † **(Genesis 3:17-18)**

That was the first time a thorn painfully pierced into the soul of humanity, but not the last.

In his second letter to the Corinthians, Paul writes about his prolonged suffering in his flesh. Like you and me, he pleaded and begged the Lord more than once to relieve him from the suffering he was experiencing.

> *"I was given a thorn in my flesh, a messenger of Satan, to torment me. Three times I pleaded with the Lord to take it away from me."* † **(2 Cor. 12:7-8 NIV)**

Paul experienced thorns. He experienced pain and suffering. As he shared the good news of the gospel, he was beaten, flogged, stoned, and had gone days without food. This thorn Paul writes about is different. It's always present. It hadn't gone away. Many scholars have researched and studied trying to figure out Paul's actual thorn. Even though there is not a definite answer to this day, many believe that Paul had permanent vision impairment due to an illness based on other things Paul wrote in his other letters in the Bible. (See Galatians 4:13-15, 6:11, Romans 16:22, Acts 23:3-5)

As we read in the book of Job, we learn that God sometimes allows the enemy to persecute and cause us pain to strengthen our faith and prove our faithfulness in Him.

---

2 Russ Ramsey. *The Advent of the Lamb of God.* (Downer's Grove, IL, InterVarsity Press, 2018) p. 26

Just as shortly after creation where the serpent weaseled himself into the world with evil trickery, thorns will be present until God's Kingdom is restored.

Jesus was not exempt from the pain of thorns while on earth, either. After Jesus had been flogged, beaten, and spit on, the soldiers put a purple royal robe on his shoulders. On his head, Jesus wore a crown made with twisted thorns by people whose hearts had also become twisted with thorns. The soldiers intentionally punctured the sharp thorns into Jesus' head. When being ridiculed, drops of blood rolled down his face like tears as the soldiers hollered to the crowd with mockery and laughter, "Hail King of the Jews!" (John 19:1-3)

That crown of thorns stayed pierced into his head as he hung on a cross. But that crown of thorns became a crown of beauty when Jesus crushed Satan to death, as his Father said would happen, back in the beginning, when He promised that to Adam and Eve and us.

Thorns in our lives should remind us of God's grace. Throughout Scripture, people feel weak due to the thorns of suffering and struggles in their lives, but Paul tells us what the Lord said to him about thorns: "My grace is enough; it's all you need. For My power is made perfect in weaknesses." (2 Cor. 12:9)

God allowed Paul to have a thorn in his life for a reason—or two or three. It could have been to keep him humble instead of prideful. It could have been a reminder of how he must depend on God's compassion. It could have been so he could use that as an example to teach us how we're made perfect in our weaknesses because of God's grace and be written and recorded in the Bible for future generations. Whatever the reason, I think that if God allows us to have a thorn in our lives, then He has something special for us to do with it.

Thorns matter. Even though we don't want them, even though they can hurt, we're given the invitation to tell our story that includes thorns. God allows them to remain as reminders of His grace for us. Our physical and mental thorns can also prompt us to recall the thorns of our suffering Lord.

Thorns cause us to feel tangled and trapped inside their rope of daily discomfort. That discomfort distorts our vision, but God sees us differently. He sees us wrapped in His love and compassion. He sees us as lovely and true. He sees the goodness in our stories that come from suffering from thorns and how they cause us to desperately depend on Jesus because He will give us enough grace and the strength we need.

And even with lingering pain, I look forward to what's in store for me: a crown of righteousness that the Lord—the always right and just Judge—will give me that day, but it is not only for me but for all those who love and long for His appearance. (2 Timothy 4:8)

Personal Reflections

What are the thorns that give you physical, emotional, or mental pain on a regular basis? Write them down, and then, take a deep breath, and say each one as you exhale. Do this for as many thorns as you can name. Hearing and feeling yourself say and release the things you suffer from may give some relief.

Do you know someone who suffers (or has suffered) from a thorn in his/her flesh? How does he/she cope with the reminding discomfort and pain? Or pray about reaching out to someone going through a similar struggle or thorn as yours. Then, share your story with that person. Knowing you're not alone can give some comfort to both of your souls.

Additional Scripture: Genesis 3:1–21, 2 Cor. 12:1–10, John 19:1–6

Personal Expressions

Go to your local grocery store that sells roses and buy yourself a bundle of them. Or if you grow them in your yard, and it's the summer season, cut some and put them in a vase where you will see them often. Be reminded of the beauty that towers over thorns, the sweet aroma of God's goodness to you.

◀) **Listen to *Crown of Thorns* by Danielle Rose**

Closing Prayer

Lord, You know this all started in the Garden of Eden when sin became part of our lives, and You told Adam that he and his descendants would live amongst thorns and thistles. Yet, Jesus, on Your head was a crown made of thorns when You were sacrificed for my sins. The land in my life has become overgrown with thorns. Even though thorns are not enjoyable, they matter because they remind me of the thorns You wore for my sins. Thank You for Your grace and the reminders of Your goodness to me. Amen.

† **(Genesis 3:18, John 19:2, Matthew 26:28, Isaiah 32:13, Psalm 27:13)**

CHAPTER 9

The Comparison Game

Opening Prayer

I confess my feelings of inadequacy, Lord. I know You have a plan for my life and You will be with me each step of the way. Amen

† **Charles Stanley** *Enter His Gates: A Daily Devotional*[1]

I do believe but help me overcome my unbelief! † **Mark 9:24**

Story

This week my goal was to write this chapter in this book. It had been a rough morning at work, and I got results from my doctor that determined I'd have to have minor surgery soon. I also heard conversations of other writers flourishing while I felt like I was in a rut, unable to think of how to begin this chapter.

While driving to our small group meeting one evening, I told my husband, "I'm thinking of quitting this writing project. I'm stuck. Anyway, I read other people's writing and mine is so elementary, it's not worth reading. I'm not good enough to publish anything. Maybe the Lord doesn't want me to write, and I misunderstood this calling."

---

1 Charles Stanley. *Enter His Gates: A Daily Devotional,* (Nashville, Thomas Nelson Publishing, 2002) p.175

The silence was loud until we rolled to a stop. My husband turned to look at me and replied, "That is not acceptable. I know God has put this assignment on your heart, and you're in the middle of it and will finish it this year. The enemy is trying to 'steal, kill, and destroy' this project you've been working on because he knows it glorifies God and will point the people who read it to the Truth. You are good enough because you and I know God is writing it through you."

Why and how do we get this lie stuck in her head: *God is good. I'm bad.* "You're not good enough" is a lie the enemy has been using since the beginning of time, especially if it has anything to do with giving God glory. I've fallen victim to that lie too many times in my life. Daily, as believers, we hear a lie in one ear, and in the other, the Truth. We hear the enemy in one ear; in the other ear is God's Spirit. In one ear, we hear, "You aren't good enough," and in the other ear, "You are good enough—I AM enough."

I AM, in other words, God has been telling us that Truth ever since He said those words to Moses.[2]

In the Bible, Moses was the Hebrew baby put in a basket and pushed down the Nile River, found by the daughter of the Pharaoh of Egypt, and raised in the palace. Once when Moses was a young man, he murdered an Egyptian who was beating a Hebrew and fled to Midian. Moses then married the daughter of the priest of Midian and became a shepherd, which he intended to be the rest of his life.

When Moses was tending his sheep on Mount Horeb, something caught his eye. As he got closer, he noticed a bush had caught on fire. Before he could even think of what to do to put the fire out, he heard a voice call his name, "Moses! Moses! Do not come any closer. Take off your sandals, for the place where you are

---

2 Exodus 3:14

standing is holy ground. I am the God of your father, the God of Abraham, the God of Isaac, and the God of Jacob."[3]

Terrified, Moses fell to the ground and covered his face, trying to grasp any understanding of what he just heard, wondering if he was dreaming. The voice of God coming from the burning bush continued to speak. "I've seen the misery of My people in Egypt who are enslaved. I've heard their cry for help, and I'm concerned about their suffering. So, I've come to rescue them, and I'm going to do that through you, Moses. I want you to go to the Pharaoh and bring My people out of Egypt."[4]

"Who, me?" Moses replied.

"I'll be with you," God said.

Moses begins elongating the conversation to stall time, still in shock, "But what if I'm asked who sent me? What do I say?"

God said to Moses, "I AM WHO I AM. This is what you're to say to the Israelites; 'I AM has sent me to you,'"[5]

Moses, still listening to the voice in the bush, spurts out his "what if" questions because the invisible enemy had invited himself into the conversation. God continued to prove to Moses that He is I AM by showing him signs or miracles that only God could do. Yet, the enemy perseveres and tells Moses that he's not good enough.

With those negative thoughts in his mind, Moses tells God,

"Oh Lord, I have never been eloquent, neither in the past nor since you have spoken to your servant. I am slow of speech and tongue. Please send someone else to do it." *I'm not good enough.*[6]

---

3   Exodus 3:4–6 paraphrased
4   Exodus 3:7–11 paraphrased
5   Exodus 3:14
6   Exodus 4:10 paraphrased

These words reside in his head: You're inadequate, unqualified, untrained, and unequipped. Is Moses the only one who's ever walked this earth who has believed those lies? No.

I'm not good enough to apply for that job. I'm not good enough to facilitate a small group at my church. I'm not good enough to befriend her. I'm not good enough to apply for that college. I'm not good enough to be a godly parent. I'm not good enough to write on a blog. I'm not good enough to be on that team. I'm not pretty enough, successful enough, smart enough, or gifted enough. I'm just not.

Do you have a "not good enough" excuse?

Have those cutting words, "I'm not good enough," sliced right through your mind, separating you from the Truth so that you'll believe the lies? The enemy is tempting us to question our God-given abilities and doubt the power of God Himself, who is the Truth. The enemy is trying to make us believe the opposite of God's Word.

God's Word says that we are sent by Him (Exodus 3:10), that the Holy Spirit gives us the words to say (Luke 12:12), that we can do all things through God who strengthens us (Philippians 4:13), that God gave us the spirit of power and love (2 Timothy 1:7), and that all things are possible for those who believe in Jesus (Mark 9:23). The enemy tries to get us to think that God doesn't speak to us and that it will never be possible to do Kingdom work adequately or effectively.

Listening to one of the pastors at our church teach recently, he said if we aren't careful, we can become consumed by the lies we tell ourselves or the lies that someone has told us in an abusive way. They bring us down and make us feel weak. Even as believers, we know we're going to heaven one day because we've confessed our sin to God and asked Him into our hearts, believing His forgiveness. Yet, at the same time, why can we think that God has no purpose or plan for our lives? When the silence speaks loud and clear, we give in to the lie and believe it's true.

One way the enemy attempts this is to get us to play The Comparison Game, where he puts thoughts or images in our head and whispers, "They're better than you." We scroll through social media sites. We look at pictures our friends and acquaintances post of all the perfect-looking-life, happy faces of family and friends, vacations, and beautifully remodeled, Pinterest-looking kitchens. Those images and stories elevate the chances of falling into the comparison game trap. When we compare ourselves to others and believe we're not as good as them, we insult God.

It's one thing to doubt or question God, but it's another to believe He's not telling the truth. When we say we aren't good enough, we're saying that what God has created is not good. God is good. (Psalm 25:8). When we disobey God and His Word, that is sin. When we choose to believe we're not good enough, we've given into the lie the enemy told us.

When we believe we're not good enough, we're struggling with our identity in Christ. God asked Moses to help His people. God asked Gideon to help His people, and He asks you and me to help His people. It's as if after Moses finally obeyed God's instructions, everybody after Moses who has said they're not good enough, God replies, "You are my Moses for this generation."[7]

In the book *Between the Dreaming and the Coming True* by Robert Benson, he wrote about this story he heard,

"Rabbi Zusya, one of the great wisdom teachers of the Hebrew tradition, once said, 'In the world to come I shall not be asked: Why were you not Moses? I shall be asked: Why were you not Zusya?"

God won't ask me, "Why weren't you, Moses? Why weren't you Queen Elizabeth? Why weren't you Beth Moore?

---

7   Robert Benson. *Between the Dreaming and the Coming True,* (Tarcher Perigee; 1st edition 2001)

God *can* ask me, though, *"Why were you not Beth Hildebrand? The only Beth Hildebrand I created you to be."*

Are you like me and can sometimes see yourself as Moses, just doing your day-to-day responsibilities, and God just shows up? He waits for us to sit with Him and have a conversation—a heart-to-heart—but we're too busy. He wants us to invite a friend who doesn't have a relationship with God to go out to lunch, but we believe what we tell her will scare her away from Jesus instead of pointing her towards Him, so we invite a friend from church instead. He wants us to volunteer some of our time in the community, but we think other people can or will, even though He wants to hear us say, "Yes, Lord, I want to serve You." But those words are still a challenge to say sometimes because we're nervous about what He'll tell us to do, so we tell Him, "I'm not good enough."

We are God's image-bearers because He created us in His image.[8] He sees us with our unique features, unique quirks, special abilities, talents, and experiences which no one else has. We were created with purpose, to reflect the fullness of God.

You are good enough to do what God created you to do and be—to reflect His glory in your own creative way. For some, it's leading people to the Promised Land. For some, it's to cook meals for the homeless. For some, it's to be a teacher. For some, it's to be a musician. For some, it's to be a Christian business owner. For some, it's to teach children (aka the next generation) in a godly way in an upside-down world. That list is endless because our purposeful God created each of us to reflect a part of Himself. So don't give up faith, don't give into lies, and don't give the enemy a seat at your table. Christ is enough! He is all we need.

You are good enough because *God is good.*

---

8 Genesis 1:27

Personal Reflections

When you're tempted to believe the damaging lie that you're not good enough to do something you know you are capable of doing, do you usually find yourself giving in to the temptation or resisting it? How? Why?

Are you discovering who you're becoming and who God created you to be in this generation? If you answer yes, describe how. If you're uncertain, pray and ask God to help you see how *you are* created in the image of God.

Additional Scripture: 1 Corinthians 1:25-31, Ephesians 1:15-23, 1 Peter 2:9-12

Personal Expressions

Here's an I AM activity for you to do. You'll need two pieces of paper (in your art journal or individual pieces), something to write with like markers, pens, colored pencils, and your Bible. In the middle of the sheet, write the words I AM on both pieces of paper. One of the I AM's is a name of God. Look through your Bible and find other names of God and write them around the I AM. You can draw lines around I AM to make it look like sunshine with the names on the rays, or however you choose. There's no right or wrong way. Then, on the other piece of paper, write I AM in the middle of the paper and this time describe characteristics about yourself based on being the image of God. For example, I AM a son or daughter, friend, encourager, survivor, God's beloved, etc. This can be a time of worship and something you can look back at when you need the reminder of Who God is and who you are in His image.

🔊 **Listen to *Redeemed* by Big Daddy Weave**

Closing Prayer

Lord, You are my Maker, my Mediator, and my Master.

Any good thing you find in me has come from you.

I want to open my mouth and taste.

Open my eyes and see how good You are.

Holy Spirit, remind me that I bear your image and heart when I forget.

I am grateful for your grace and goodness. Amen.

† **(Psalm 16:2, Psalm 34:8)**

CHAPTER 10

Be Loved

Opening Prayer

Now, to God the Father, who first loved us, and made us accepted in the Beloved; to God the Son, who loved us, and washed us from our sins in his own blood; to God the Holy Ghost, who sheddeth the love of God abroad in our hearts, be all love and all glory in time and to all eternity. Amen. † **John Wesley**[1]

I am my lover's, and my lover is mine. † **Song of Songs 6:3**

Story

In the middle of our grassy backyard sat a three-tiered pedestal, like the one Olympic athlete stand on during a medal ceremony. With my shoulders slumped and my face looking down, I stood on the highest level of the platform and placed a rusty crown with a gold, shiny letter "L" protruding from its base. The "L" did not represent the initial of my first or last name. It did not represent words like "lovely" or even "likable."

The "L" stood for "Loser."

That's the prestigious award I gave myself.

---

1 John Wesley, 1703–1791

Of course, this took place in my imagination as sweat rolled down my face on that humid, unseasonably hot spring afternoon. My husband tilled the ground in our garden, preparing it for me to plant the little seedlings he'd nurtured in our garage during the winter. I enjoy admiring the flowers and veggies from our window and on our kitchen table, but planting and taking care of them is not my favorite hobby. Every year it's my job to dig tiny holes, add fertilizer, gently put the baby plant in its new home, and fill the gap back up with dirt.

I collected my gardening tools and made my way to the garden. Sweat instantly dripped off my forehead into the small holes where I put the baby plants. What seemed like an hour later, I picked up the tools and empty containers and headed back to the garage. Across the yard, beside the garage door, sat a white bag with a picture of a bouquet of flowers. *Oh no.* I completely forgot the fertilizer that helps the plant roots grow!

There was a time when I would have laughed at myself or shrugged my shoulders, but not this time.

Instead of laughing about it, I lost it.

I made my way over to the pedestal in my mind, with the "L" crown on my head. I burst out in anger at myself and towards my husband. *What a forgetful and messed-up person I am. I get the Loser crown. I don't do anything right; I always make these dumb mistakes.*

Have you ever put yourself on a pedestal in your mind, being crowned with a large "L" on your head? I hope not, but there's someone I know who has.

It's a label we sometimes think is true because the evil one strategically knows how to make us doubt our worth and believe lies that tear us down emotionally, mentally, and even physically.

The reason I described myself as a loser is because that slivering serpent in my garden whispered lies to me that afternoon, and

I believed them. I must have because it was such a petty reason to get upset. In that moment of forgetfulness, I heard, "You're a bad mom, wife, sister, daughter, friend, mentor, and leader. You can't even do something as simple as sprinkling dust in the ground."

I wished I could crawl into one of those holes in the ground.

Later that day, I spent some time in our sunroom. I sat, staring into nowhere.

"Lord, please help me," I whispered. "Please help me!" I begged. "I know Your Word says You'll never leave me, and there's goodness that can come from the struggle I'm going through right now, but I simply want to enjoy life again. I'm tired of being low."

As loud as silence can be, God whispered to me, "Beloved."

Beloved?

Or was it, "Be loved"?

Or maybe it was both.

A still, small voice inside of me said, "You are My beloved—so allow yourself to be loved." I am HIS beloved—so allow myself to be loved."

If I'm His beloved, I need to allow myself to be loved.

Deep down, I knew many people liked me and a few more who loved me, but one person did not like me—that person was me. I felt like a dried-up plant for over two years. Self-rejection grew like a weed and took over the good soil surrounding my heart. It was as if that serpent planted the seeds of the weeds that grew into ugly lies that sound like, "You're not good enough. God is ignoring you. He isn't helping you like you're asking Him to. How can you believe He loves you?"

In his book, *Life of the Beloved: Spiritual Living in a Secular World*, Henri J. M. Nouwen penned these words:

*"Self-rejection is the greatest enemy of the spiritual life because
it contradicts the sacred voice that calls us the 'Beloved.' Being
the Beloved expresses the core truth of our existence."*[2]

Later that afternoon, I started digging again—this time into the
pages of my Bible. I discovered my NIV Bible included the word
"beloved" only three times, but two caught my attention.

"I am my Beloved's and my beloved is mine" (Song of Songs 6:3),—
I'll come back to that in a minute.

And,

"Let the beloved of the Lord rest secure in him, for he shields
her all day long, and the one the Lord loves rests between his
shoulders." (Deuteronomy 33:12)

So, what is significant about that? Right before he died, Moses
blessed each of Israel's tribes. He encouraged and motivated
them to continue in obedience and love for the Lord as they
entered the Promised Land on the horizon. They had been
wandering for 40 years, and their leader, whom they respected
and followed, was about to die. The blessing above is the one
Moses gave to the tribe called Benjamin. As a little reminder,
Benjamin was Judah's youngest son and the well-known
Joseph's younger and only blood-related brother. After Joseph's
older brothers sold him as a slave, they lied to their father and
told him wild animals killed him. From that point on, Benjamin
became Judah's favorite son. Then years later, twelve tribes were
created and appointed within the nation of Israel, each of them
named after Judah's sons.

Maybe that's why Moses called Benjamin's tribe the Lord's
beloved. The origin of the word *beloved* comes from the Greek
word *yedid*, which means "(well) loved" or, as we understand today,
dear, favorite, or *worthy of love*.) Moses used the word *yedid* to

---

2   Henri J. Nouwen. *Life of the Beloved: Spiritual Living in a Secular World*, (New York:
The Crossroad Publishing Company 10th Edition 2002)

express how deeply the Lord loved them as if they were his favorite tribe. They were instructed to rest on the Lord's shoulders.

It had been a long 40 years, which God knew. Even more, the Lord wanted His people to know that He would carry them on His shoulders then and in the generations after them. Not only did God speak that promise through Moses, but also through Isaiah when he prophesied, "For to us a child is born, to us, a son is given, and the government will be on his shoulders." (Isaiah 9:6) Then, 750 years later, Jesus' disciples witnessed the Lord tell His Son, Jesus, a couple of different times, "This is my beloved Son with whom I am well-pleased; listen to Him!" Ultimately, Jesus showed us how He'd carry our sins on his shoulders, as He carried a cross on them so we can see how much He loves us. And because of His love, we are worthy.

God called His Son Jesus His Beloved, and He calls you and me His beloved, too. God does not require us to love Him back. But He sure wants to make sure we know He loves us. God desires us to know without a doubt that He loves us, and other people love us also. We are to live like Jesus, and Jesus loves people, including himself, because he emulated his Father, and his Father loves him. So today, just as it says in the book of Deuteronomy, the Lord promises He will carry each one of us when we cannot put one foot in front of the other.

The next day, I just so happened to have a scheduled meeting with Fil Anderson, a spiritual director and author I meet with occasionally. I told him about my struggle with loving myself, much less liking myself during that time. Instead of giving me a list of suggestions to help me sort through my struggles, he told me a story of a time in his life where he had a similar experience. What got him through that season was one sentence in Song of Songs 6:3

He spoke those words to me with compassion, "I am my Beloved's, and my beloved is mine."

Fil then reached over to a bowl on a table in his office, placed something in his hand, and reached out his arm, putting it in my hand. Not knowing what it was, I opened my hand, and in it, he had placed a small, wooden cross, called a pocket cross.

He then said, "I needed that reminder, so every time I looked in the mirror, I imagined those words tattooed on my forehead so I wouldn't forget that God *loves* me. When you get home, I want you to write that verse on this cross with a Sharpie pen—*I am my Beloved's, and my beloved is mine.* Whenever you put your hand in your pocket, pull it out and read it to remind yourself that *you* are God's beloved. Because you are."

Fil had no idea I had read those exact words the day before, searching for the word 'beloved' in the Bible. When I was back home, I searched through the junk drawer in the kitchen to find a Sharpie and wrote those words on my cross, and thanked God. As I prayed, it was as if God whispered to me again, this time saying, "You know, I'd like you to wear that 'L' crown you put on your head yesterday, but the 'L' no longer stands for 'loser.' Now the 'L' stands for 'LOVED.' I no longer want you to *be low* and believe the lies you hear. Instead, I long for you to know that you are loved, My *beloved*."

Friend, if you too sometimes put on that imaginary "L" crown, "L" stands for "LOVED." You are loved by God. Deeply. You are worthy of love. You are God's beloved.

Let yourself, the Lord's favorite, rest secure in Him. He shields you all day long, and you, the one the Lord loves, rest on His shoulders.

You are His beloved, so allow yourself to be loved.

Personal Reflections

Make a list of lies you have told yourself about yourself. Next, besides those lies, write the opposite of those lies. Now, take some time searching through the Bible and what God says about those lies and truths you listed.

Make a list of specific times when you felt loved. For example, how does it make you feel to hear and know God loves you?

Additional Scripture: Matthew 12:15–18, Psalm 119:25–32, 1 John 4:7–19

Personal Expressions

Write on something like a smooth piece of wood or a stone you can fit in your pocket, "You are my Beloved's, and my beloved is mine" with a permanent pen. Keep it close and be reminded who you are—God's beloved.

🔊 **Listen to *Lift My Eyes* by Bebo Norman**

Closing Prayer

My Beloved, You show me Your unfailing love in wonderful ways. By Your mighty power, You rescue those who seek refuge from their enemies. Save me! Rescue me from the power of my enemies because their mouths are full of lies; they swear to tell the truth, but they lie instead. Help me not to be captured by those lies. God, Your Word says that blessed are those who patiently endure testing and temptation. Afterward, they will receive the crown of life that You have promised to those who love You. Lord, You are my Beloved, and I am Yours. Amen.

† (Psalm 17:7, Psalm 144:11, Psalm 59:12, James 1:12, Song of Solomon 6:3)

CHAPTER 11

Forgotten

Opening Prayer

O Christ Jesus,
when all is darkness
and we feel our weakness and helplessness,
give us the sense of your presence,
Your love, and your strength.
Help us to have perfect trust
in your protecting love
and strengthening power,
so that nothing may frighten or worry us,
for, living close to you,
we shall see your hand,
Your purpose, your will through all things.

† St. Ignatius of Loyola

Then Pilate turned Jesus over to them to be crucified. So, they took Jesus away. Carrying the cross by himself, he went to the place called Place of the Skull (in Hebrew, Golgotha). There they nailed him to the cross. Two others were crucified with him, one on either side, with Jesus between them. **† John 19:16–18**

Story

The whiff of ink, oil paint, and paint thinner hit me as soon as I stepped into the room: stained paintbrushes, tin cans, and plastic cups splattered with crusted paint clutter the messy counters. The dull, cream-and-gray walls contrast with bold colors, which brings the room to life. Several square and rectangle pieces of paper hang on the walls or propped up on easels around the room.

A group of artificial fruit and a plant sits on one of the tables, along with a statue of an ancient nude man and some boxes covered by an old blanket to give height and depth. But, looking past this, what caught my eye was a large, sturdy table with a big wheel attached to what looked like an elongated and enlarged empty roll of paper towels. It was a printmaking machine.

My college senior art project was an exhibit of different styles of printmaking: monotype, linocut, silkscreen, and engraving prints. The subject matter for my project: people with many wrinkles. To make a print on this machine, the artist rolls ink on a piece of plexiglass, metal, or wood, then covers it with a damp piece of paper, and sends it under the heavy roller on the printing machine, as the artist turns the wheel. After the rolling is complete and the paper peeled off the machine, an impression, or print, is revealed of whatever was on the plexiglass, metal, or wood.

The processes I chose for my project took more time than antici-pated, but I accepted the challenge. The countless hours I spent in the studio became my escape as I worked on making impressions. Even though I had already learned much about art, techniques, mediums, and art history, there was still much to learn, including the art of engraving, which turned out to be the style of most of my finished pieces displayed in my senior exhibit.

Here's a little art lesson for you. When it comes to engraving, there are two different types: relief prints or intaglio prints. Relief printing is when the space around the image the artist wants to be printed is removed from the wood or metal. Before printing, the artist applies ink to the raised image, then rolls it under the machine's pressure. The ink on the surface will appear on the paper. An example of this is rubber stamps of your address that you stamp on the envelopes you mail out.

Intaglio printing is the opposite of relief printing, where an indented space on a zinc or copper plate or panel is filled with paint and then run through the pressing machine. This process happens when the artist uses a burin scraping tool to form an image. Liquid acid is then applied to the panel that eats away the surface, causing a depression called etching. After rolling paint over the panel, it's then rubbed off with a cloth, leaving paint in the crevasses. Then, paper is placed on top of the panel, rolled under the printing machine's pressure, resulting in the depressed imprint appearing on the paper.

The oldest engraved piece of art found by archeologists, titled *Bison with Turned Head*, sits in a museum in France (It's easy to find an image of it on the internet). Through studies, the age of this relic is 15,000 BC. Yes, that's correct, before Christ. This piece of art was engraved on a spear-thrower, a weapon made from a reindeer antler. This artist understood incising or carving techniques when you see the delicate incisions.[1]

About 13,500 years later, when Moses walked this earth while leading the Israelites to the Promised Land, he had the opportunity to do some engraving himself. God told Moses to write the 10 Commandments on two stones.

---

1   Horst De La Croix, Richard G. Tansey, Diane Kirkpatrick, *Art Through the Ages: Ancient, Medieval, and Non-European Art*, 9th Edition (New York: Harcourt Brace College Publishers, 1991) p. 35

"The Lord said to Moses, 'Chisel out two stone tablets like the first ones, and I will write on them the words that were on the first tablets, which you broke '...and he wrote on the tablets the words of the covenant—the Ten Commandments."

† **(Exodus 34:1 and 28)**

(He must have had nice handwriting because it had to be readable by others. It makes me wonder if pretty doodles decorated the corners or edges. I don't think God would've minded it because He's an Artist Himself.)

But what I want us to focus on here is about 700 years later, when God uses beautiful imagery of engraving, when He tells Isaiah the words to write to His beloved people who were in exile. The Babylonians had conquered and captured the people in the nation of Judah who had chosen to ignore God's instructions and sinned against Him, turning their backs to God. Because of their decisions and actions against Him, there were consequences, and God allowed Babylon to raid Judah, including God's temple, and took the people captive. (2 Kings 24:10–17)

The people had been suffering living under Babylonian rule, and God once again extended His grace and compassion when the people cried out to Him. The Lord then said,

"'Shout for joy, O heavens; rejoice, O earth; burst into song, O mountains! For the Lord comforts his people and will have compassion on his afflicted ones.'

But Zion (God's people) said, 'The Lord has forsaken me, the Lord has forgotten me.'

'Can a mother forget the baby at her breast and have no compassion on the child she has borne? Though she may forget, I will not forget you! See, I have engraved you on the palms of my hands.'" (Isaiah 49:13–16a NIV)

Go back and read the lament the people of Zion cried out. Does the response of God's people sound familiar? Not only because this isn't the first time it had happened in Scripture, but have you ever said those words?

"The Lord has forgotten me."

I still have cancer. Our house was flooded and destroyed from a hurricane months ago, and we still do not have a place to call home. I was furloughed from my job, and I still cannot find another one, and I'm at the end of my savings. It's as if our son has disowned us, and we've done all we can to reach out to him and pray for his return, but nothing has changed. My husband and I have tried everything, including counseling, and our marriage isn't getting better. I've been on an emotional rollercoaster, and I cannot feel the peace of God. I pray, read the Bible, journal, listen to Christian podcasts, and attend church every weekend, and I still can't seem to connect with Jesus. If you allow those struggles to sit too long, its bitter acidity can cut deeply through your soul, leaving you in a sunken hole that allows more sorrow to collect and distort the beauty of God's masterpiece.

God has not forgotten about you. Yes, there are times when it might feel like God has forgotten about you. There are times when His presence feels absent, and you feel alone. But, remember and believe He has not. I know for a fact that there have been too many times when I've had spiritual amnesia and forgotten God and His Truth. The only thing God forgets is our confessed and repented sins. God does not need help to remember, yet He still chooses to engrave your name on the palm of His hand. God's Spirit is telling you right this minute that YOU—yes, you— are engraved in the palm of God's hand.

Recently I've been reading the sermons and writings of Charles H. Spurgeon, a preacher in the late 1800's. In his November 7, 1868 devotion in his book, *Mornings and Evenings,* Spurgeon writes about us being written on the palm of God's hand.

Spurgeon quoted the King James Version of Isaiah 49:16, "I have graven *thee.*" In today's language, it reads: "God says, 'I have engraved *you.*' And yes, *you* refers to Jerusalem, or Zion, the eternal community of believers, as we see in Isaiah 49:14. But God declares His Word is relevant to each person who has ever lived and will ever live. A community or city is made up of individual people. So, the *you* can be said to you and me. When I think of that promise written in Scripture, that 'I have engraved you,' I think about how He did not say, 'I have engraved *your name* on the palm of my hand.'

Of course, your name is part of who you are, but there's something deeper when the Lord uses the word 'you.' The Lord is saying, "I have engraved, or tattooed, *your* name, *your* image, *your* circumstances, *your* passions, *your* quirks, *your* talents, *your* weakness, *your* wants, *your* works—everything about *you*—on My hand. So how can God forget about you when He has engraved *you* upon His own palm?"[2]

Now, in the palm of Jesus' hands are the scars—not from just a shallow scratch or indention from an artist's tool—but from large, iron nails hammered all the way through his hands to the wooden cross. How can those scars be beautiful when they're a reminder of the suffering and pain he experienced on the cross? Maybe it's because when he sees his scars on the palms of his hands, he's reminded of beautiful you and me and how much he loves us as he sits beside his Father, Who has all of us engraved in the palm of His hand. He did not write our names on His hand with chalk, charcoal, or paint that easily washes off.[3] He wants us tattooed on Himself because He really loves us.

Friend, may you always remember that God has chiseled you on the palm of His hand, and may His Truth be engraved on your heart. May the punctures and pains you're feeling become beauty scars you're not ashamed to show, and may you believe that you indeed are a masterpiece of God.

---

2   Charles H. Spurgeon. "Morning/Evening Reading: *Blue Letter Bible*, https://www.blueletterbible.org/devotionals/me/view.cfm?Date=11/07&Time=both&body=1

3   "Isaiah 49:16–Inscribed on His Hands." *Precept Austin*, 24 December 2016, https://www.preceptaustin.org/inscribed_on_his_hands

Personal Reflections

Do you feel the pull of the temptation to question God's goodness toward you by thinking He's forgotten about you? First, name and write down your doubts, or unbelief's, you've been carrying. Then write the opposite of that doubt or unbelief and find Scripture to confirm the truth God wants and desires you to believe.

Today, are you experiencing punctures or pain in your heart or soul—an addiction, anger, impatience, greed, lies on feeling unworthy, an underlying sin? Name it. Write it down. Then pray, asking God for the discomfort to be Him chiseling it to form you more into His image, His beautiful masterpiece.

Additional Scripture: Isaiah 49, Exodus 34, 2 Corinthians 3

Personal Expressions

Experiment with a fun engraving technique called Crayon Etching. Look on your electronic device or in a library for "simple crayon etching projects" and enjoy the process.

◀)) **Listen to** *God Has Not Forgot* **by Tonex**

Closing Prayer

Lord, I want to delight in Your decrees and not forget Your word and promises. I sing for joy and rejoice in You because You have compassion for those who suffer and will never forget about us, leaving us alone. Please help me to remember that

I am tattooed to the palm of Your hand. Your Son said that even sparrows are not forgotten, which means You will never forget me either. I must nail my passions and desires of sinful nature on the cross and crucify them there. I pray that each generation will set its hope anew on You, not forgetting Your glorious miracles and obeying Your commands. Amen

**† (Psalm 119:16, Isaiah 49:13–16, Luke 12:6,
Galatians 5:24, Psalm 78:7)**

CHAPTER 12

Numb and Know

Opening Prayer

My Father, I've been struggling within because of some of the places life has led me...and struggling with you too...I come to you today, Father, and ask you to begin refreshing and nourishing my soul again.

† Amy Carmichael: *Come Quietly to Meet You*[1]

*Let me hear your promise of blessing over my life,
breaking me free from the proud oppressors.
As a lovesick lover, I yearn for more of your salvation
and for your virtuous promises.
Let me feel your tender love, for I am yours.
Give me more understanding of your wonderful ways.
I need more revelation from your Word
to know more about you, for I'm in love with you!
Lord, the time has come for you to break through...*

† Psalm 119:122–126a (TPT)

---

1   Amy Carmichael. *Come Quietly to Meet You: An Intimate Journey In God's Presence,* (Minneapolis, MN: Bethany House, 1991) p. 60

Story

I felt burned out.

Then it turned into grieving the loss of my dad due to cancer.

Then depression sank in.

All that time, though, God and I were still tight. I talked with Him daily, asked Him many questions, read His Love Letter, even sang worship songs despite not sounding very good at it.

I believed that I'd snap out of this season of depression like I have the few other times earlier in my life. But days turned into weeks, weeks turned into months, and months turned into a year. And with each day that passed, with no improvement, I began to believe that God stepped away, and I had no idea when or if He'd come back. I had been asking Him to heal me from my brainsickness countless times, and with no response from Him, I felt I had lost any sense of God's presence in my life.

I told myself there must be more important things God needed to tend to instead of being with me. I questioned what I had done wrong. I told myself lies (and believed them) that I didn't have enough faith and had to prove myself to God before He'd be willing to answer my prayer. Ever since I had given my heart to God, I had never felt or believed those thoughts. I had never mistrusted God or toyed with the idea that He'd abandon me. Why now? I had heard other people's stories who experienced that, but I never thought that would happen to me.

All I wanted was to feel His love and compassion for my broken heart and spirit within my heart and soul.

Even though my emotions had taken control of my brain, something significant had been stored in it—the facts.

If you're like me, you may have experienced a time when you suffered from the feeling of being separated from God and His love for you. When you feel the sting of rejection, the ache of loneliness, or fear of abandonment, those hurts can make it hard to think clearly. These emotions are powerful because we long for intimacy that's not there. Our feelings make it hard to believe the Truth about God. Even though it isn't easy, friend, do not give up on Him.

We feel negative emotions because we are flesh. We are humans. We get sick—physically, emotionally, mentally. We have different moods, challenging circumstances, and hormones. When we're in those difficult moments or years, there's one thing I've learned the long and hard way—you must rely on the facts rather than your feelings. A fact is a fact.

God, the Good Shepherd, never stops loving you, tenderly and compassionately, even if you don't *feel* it. The factual evidence is in His Love Letter to you—the Bible.

In 1 John 4:9-10, John tells us, "This is how God *showed* his love among us: He sent His one and only Son into the world that we might live through Him. This is love: not that we loved God, but that He loved us and sent His Son as an atoning sacrifice for our sins."

John didn't say, "This is how God showed His love for us; He answered all our prayers the way we wanted them answered, He gave us a perfect spouse, child, or parent, He made sure we'd never be discouraged, or He'd never allow us to suffer or go through pain, anxiety, or depression." If God showed us His love by doing everything we desired, we would never feel the *need* for His presence and love in our lives.

If anyone who ever lived can relate to not feeling God's love and presence, it's Jesus. More than anyone, all his life, he had a deep relationship with God, our Father. Even during his demanding schedule of teaching his disciples and crowds of people through-out his ministry, Jesus maintained communication and intimacy with the Lord.

That changed, though, the night He was arrested by the Pharisees. As Jesus was taken to court, beaten, flogged, carried a cross, was nailed to that cross, and hung from it, He experienced the feeling of being abandoned by God. While hanging on the cross, as blood poured out of the cuts all over his body from razored whips, He struggled to take a deep enough breath to call out, "My God, my God, why have You forsaken me?" (Matthew 27:46)

Yet after Jesus moaned those words, thinking of the past 24 horrific hours of his life, he knew God is who He says He is. He knew God's truth, promises, and reason for allowing this to happen. In his humanness, Jesus precisely experienced what we may have felt– absolutely alone and abandoned by God. Deep down in his bones, though, he knew God still loved him. Jesus showed us his love by absorbing our sins and dying on the cross for us to have eternal life with him. He wanted more than anything for us to be with him in heaven. He had just prayed to God out loud with his disciples at their last supper together.

I can imagine hearing Jesus almost plead to God, "Father, I want those You have given me to be with me where I am, and to see my glory, the glory You have given me because You loved me before the creation of the world." (John 17:24)

That is a fact that will never change. Jesus yearns for you to be where he is. Those were His words; we can count on them. That truth cannot be taken away from our souls.

Our brains are amazing, complex organs God so intricately formed which scientists are still learning new things about them. One discovery is how we have two hemispheres in our brain— the right and left. The left side allows us to have logic, reason, and language. The right side of our brain controls creativity, innovation, and our emotions.

Deep within the right side of our brain, where our emotions live, is the root of our ability to trust—a vital part of our body, mind, and soul. Trust is complete confidence, fearing nothing in someone or something. Trust is absolute confidence in God, fearing nothing. So when we're going through a low season, that is when the right side of our brains can exercise.

Curt Thomas, a psychiatrist, who has researched and written about the phenomenal link between neuroscience, spirituality, and the Bible, has much insight into our brains and emotions. He states, "Left–brain mental processing disregards the right–brain emotional elements of trust that are necessary for life to thrive. When I know that I know something because I can logically prove it, I step away from trust."[2]

When we suffer from emotionlessness to God's love, we must have gut trust in Him. We must trust what we know about Him through His Word. Trusting God is a form of worship. You may not be in a mood to sing praise to God, to pray, or even open your Bible, but if the only thing you're motivated to do is trust Him, then trust Him. And when you do, that brings Him glory.

In his book, *Ruthless Trust,* Brennon Manning wrote, "Why does our trust offer such immense pleasure to God? Because trust is the preeminent expression of love. Thus, it may mean more to Jesus when we say, 'I trust You,' than when we say, 'I love you.'"[3]

Trusting the facts of God's Word even when you don't feel His presence in your life is an act of faith and an act of worship. So while I was reading *Ruthless Trust* for the first time, I scribbled these decisions in the back of it:

I'll trust God that goodness will eventually come from this dark season of life.

I'll trust God that the past two years will have taught me something.

---

2   Curt Thompson. *Anatomy of the Soul: Surprising Connections between neuroscience and spiritual practices that can transform your life and relationships* (Illinois: Tyndale House Publishers, 2010) p. 8–9
3   Brennon Manning. *Ruthless Trust* (New York: HarperOne:HarperCollins Publishers, 2002) p. 180–181

I'll trust God that this time of depression will one day turn into joy.

I'll trust God that I'll somehow be able to minister to others struggling and battling from an internal struggle.

I'll trust God that He never left my side and has carried me through this, even though I don't feel like He has. Maybe it's because His weight of glory is so light, I can't recognize it.

I'll trust God's power and grace for me.

I'll trust God that He really does continue to call me His beloved.

I'll trust God's promises in the Bible.

I also sometimes say to myself, "I know, that I know, that I know..."

Say that out loud for yourself: "I know, that I know, that I know."

Know the kind of extravagant love the Father has lavished on you. (1 John 3:1)

Know God through His Word because it's true and trustworthy. (2 Timothy 3:16)

Know God has you covered on all sides—on the right, the left, above, below, in front, and from the back. (Psalm 139:5)

Know God's Spirit does live in you, and He will never abandon you even if you don't feel it. Know it. Trust His Word. "You have to decide to trust the Voice that says, 'I love you.'"[4]

And one day, you will feel Him again.

---

4   Brennon Manning. *Ruthless Trust* (New York: HarperOneHarperCollins Publishers, 2002) p. 21

Personal Reflections

Do you find it a challenge or not to feel God's love for you? Why do you think that is or how?

 If you're struggling from not feeling the love of God in your life right now, write a list of areas in which you will choose to trust God. If you feel the presence of God in your life, write a list of the ways or how you experience that feeling.

Additional Scripture: Jeremiah 17:5–8, 1 John 2:12–14, Romans 5:3–5

Personal Expressions

Curt Thompson, mentioned above, teaches more about our right and left hemispheres related to David's psalms. Referring to Psalm 51, Thompson writes, "David does not dictate a theological treatise on adultery and the proper place of confession and absolution. He does not mechanically utter some prefabricated prayer. Instead, he writes poetry. He stands up to his full emotional height, and in this psalm, accomplishes the integration of the right and left hemispheres of his brain. This what poetry does."

Now you're challenged to exercise both sides of your brain and write your own poem. First, write what you know about God or trust in God (it doesn't have to rhyme!) and then offer it as worship to the Lord.

◄)) **Listen to *I Will Trust My Savior Jesus* by CityAlight**

Closing Prayer

Today, God, I am choosing to trust that You have extravagant love You lavish on me. You know that sometimes I don't feel it, yet I know, that I know, that I know You still love me. I choose to believe that because of Your great power, when I'm pressed on every side by troubles, I will not be crushed. When I am perplexed, I will not be driven to despair. When I am hunted down, You will never abandon me. You will never allow me to be passed into my enemy's hands when I get knocked down. Through suffering, my body continues to share in the death of Your Son, Jesus, so that the life of Jesus will also be seen in me. Thank You for the wealth of your grace and kindness to me. Amen.

† (1 John 3:1, 2 Corinthians 4:7-10, Ephesians 2:7)

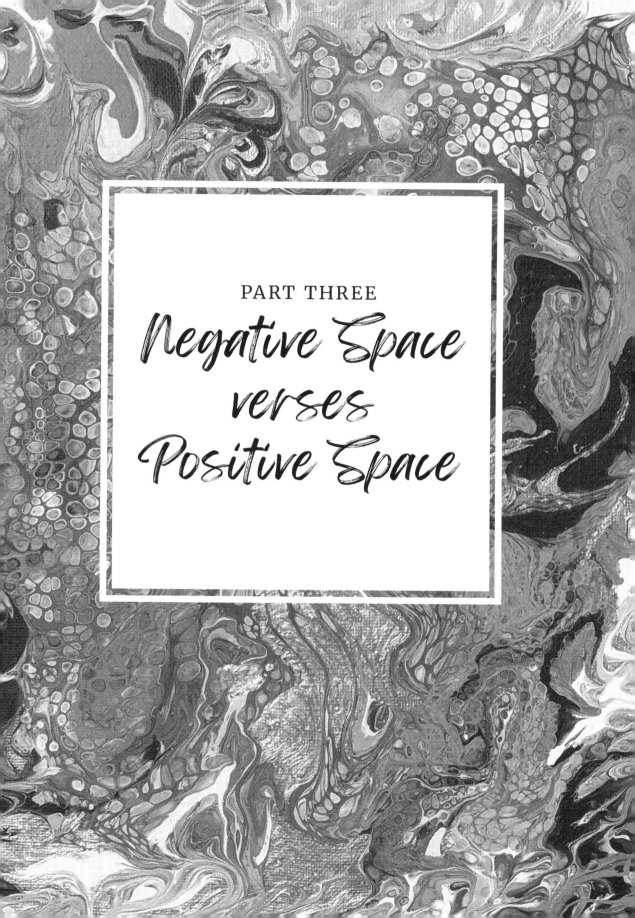

PART THREE

Negative Space
verses
Positive Space

CHAPTER 13

It's OK To Lament

Opening Prayer

May we be a people who aren't afraid to cry out to the Father in times of great need. May we, like David, place our trust in the one who is with all of us in our grief. And, may we be a people who come alongside the hurting—even if all we can offer is a warm embrace and a listening ear.

† Ed Stetzer, executive director of the Wheaton College Billy Graham Center[1]

He has made me chew on gravel.
He has rolled me in the dust.
Peace has been stripped away,
and I have forgotten what prosperity is.
I cry out, "My splendor is gone!
Everything I had hoped for from the Lord is lost!"

The thought of my suffering and homelessness
is bitter beyond words.
I will never forget this awful time,
as I grieve over my loss.
Yet I still dare to hope
when I remember this:

---

1 Ed Stetzer. "Recovering the Good in Seasons of Lament." 14 September 2020, https://edstetzer.com/blog/recovering-the-good-in-seasons-of-lament

The faithful love of the Lord never ends!
His mercies never cease.
Great is his faithfulness;
his mercies begin afresh each morning.
I say to myself, "The Lord is my inheritance;
therefore, I will hope in him!" † **Lamentations 3:16-24**

Story

Lord, just like people must have water to survive, I need You to survive. I have countlessly asked You to relieve me from my sadness and loneliness, but You haven't. It just seems to have gotten worse, and I don't know how much longer I can go on feeling this way.

I want and need to delight in You again, Lord, but it's hard. Still. I can't seem to delight in anything. I beg to have the intimate relationship I had with You a few months ago. Have I been deaf to your comfort, or have You been silent to me? The evil one has a tight grip, and I feel too weak to fight, and I don't feel You fighting for me, but I will and must trust that You are.

I choose to still lift You high, oh Sovereign God, and glorify Your Name. Amen.

I scribbled my prayer of lament in my journal several years ago when I was battling a bout of depression. I once heard the Bible called "the record of human sorrows," As you read through the Bible and this book, we're going to see many people who experienced sorrow, grief, sadness, or despair at some point in their lives. Just like us. Just think about that for a minute.

As believers, there's a difference between lament and the negative thoughts of anger or sorrow every single person naturally feels. The difference is that lament is a prayer instead of a moment of rage where we say and do things we may later regret. Lament includes God, and these types of prayers are woven throughout the Bible as powerful and poetic works of art.

In the book *Lamentations and The Tears Of The World*, Kathleen M. O'Connor beautifully describes lamentations like this:

> *"Laments are prayers that erupt from wounds, burst out of unbearable pain, and bring it to language. Laments complain, shout, and protest. They take anger and despair before God and the community. They grieve. They argue. They find fault. Without complaint, there is no lament form...They cry out that life is unbearable, suffering too great, and the future hopeless... But remarkably, in the process of harsh complaint and resistance, they also express faith in God in the midst of chaos, doubt, and confusion."*[2]

Jeremiah is the author of the book Lamentations in the Bible. He is crying out to God, literally weeping, after God allowed the holy city, Jerusalem, to be destroyed by the Babylonians. As a result, many Jewish people were killed, including their king, and the remaining people left in exile. Jeremiah had warned them if they didn't change their ungodly ways, punishment would come, and in their rejection of God's Word spoken to them by way of Jeremiah, the people suffered greatly. Lamentations reveal a tragic story of deep suffering on a large scale, but the Bible offers us a more intimate look at personal suffering in the story of Job.

Job was "blameless—a man of complete integrity. He feared God and stayed away from evil."[3] God really liked him. Satan didn't, though, and challenged God to let him test Job. Satan told God that he knows God has been protecting and blessing Job, but if all of Job's belongings and people he loved were taken away from him, then Job would curse God and turn away from Him. God accepted the challenge by saying, "All right, you may test

---

2   Kathleen M. O'Connor. *Lamentations and The Tears of the World,* (New York: Orbis Books, 2002) p. 9
3   Job 1:1

him. Do whatever you want with everything he possesses, but don't harm him physically."[4] And Satan accepted the challenge.

Shortly after that, Job's animals were raided, his farm helpers killed, and his barns set ablaze. The wind tore down his home, which also killed all his children. Yet when his wife and friends told Job to curse God because of all that had happened, Job replied, "'Should we accept only good things from the hand of God and never anything bad?' So, in all this, Job said nothing wrong."

"Job said nothing wrong." When you read the book of Job, you'll also discover how Job wailed, cried out, and may have said Hebrew curse words, but he never once cursed God Himself. He lamented these words in the book of Job:

Why wasn't I born dead? (3:11)

If my misery could be weighed and my troubles be put on the scales, they would outweigh all the sands of the sea. (6:2)

O God, remember that my life is but a breath, and I will never again feel happiness. (7:7)

You formed me with your hands; you made me, yet now you completely destroy me. (10:8)

And now my life seeps away. Depression haunts my days. At night my bones are filled with pain, which gnaws at me relentlessly. With a strong hand, God grabs my shirt. He grips me by the collar of my coat. He has thrown me into the mud. I'm nothing more than dust and ashes. (30:16–19).

And that is just a smidge of the complaints Job cried out to God and others. Then, finally, God's silence ends, and he comes to Job continuing to challenge him by asking him many questions he knew Job wouldn't be able to answer, reminding Job of Who God is—God of the universe.

---

4 Job 1:12

Job continued to cry out to the Lord, this time in repentance and praise, even when he was still suffering. "You (God) said, 'Listen, and I will speak! I have some questions for You, and You must answer them.' I had only heard about You before, but now I have seen You with my own eyes. So I take back everything I said, and I sit in dust and ashes to show my repentance." Job was also displaying his praise to God through action.

As mentioned, lamenting is a poetic form of art that began in ancient times and is still practiced today, although you may not realize it. There are many things to lament, such as wounds, pain, corruption, poverty, injustice, abuse, doubt, and death. The physical, spiritual, and mental troubles that we battle can begin to heal when we express our honest emotions to God in lament. Have you ever noticed that the same letters in the word *lament* are also in the word *mental*? Even when we have physical issues, mental challenges become intertwined with them. Our minds begin to react with an emotion, which is what they were designed to do. It's our choice how we respond—in retaliation or lamentation. Lament is part of having a healthy mental life.

Often, we don't realize we need to lament. You might think you don't know how to lament because you're not a poet. Here is a way that might help you get started. You can do this while praying aloud, silently, or writing in your journal. This format is evident in Psalm 13.

Confront God. Call out his name and invite Him into the conversation. "*O Lord, how long will you forget me? Forever? How long will you look the other way?*" (13:1)

Complain to God. Now's the time to complain to God all that's on your heart and mind. You can be as raw and gut-honest as you want to be because you're in the presence of God, and He's listening and even knows your thoughts before you do. "*How long must I struggle with anguish in my soul, with sorrow in my heart every day? How long will my enemy have the upper hand?*" (13:2)

Call out to God. Call out boldly for God to help even if you're still upset, angry, or hurt. He still loves you and always wants you to run to Him no matter what you've done or how you feel. *"Turn and answer me, O Lord my God! Restore the sparkle to my eyes, or I will die. Don't let my enemy gloat, saying, 'We have defeated him!' Don't let them rejoice at my downfall."* (13:3–4)

Count on God's Sovereignty. Now it's time to tell God that you'll trust Him. Trust is the distinction and beauty of lamentations. Sometimes it's not easy to understand His ways, but trusting Him is worth it. Surrender and obedience to God are always worth it. David shows his trust by saying, *"But I trust in Your unfailing love."* (13:5a)

Continue to praise God. End your prayer of lament with words of affirmation and declaration of Who God is. *"I will rejoice because you have rescued me. I will sing to the Lord because He is good to me."* (13:5b–6).

We can lament because we know God is good and His heart is gentle towards us. When we have a relationship with someone, especially a deep one, both reveal their deep emotions—both positive and negative. Yes, God is Sovereign and the Creator of all things, and He's also personable and loves you—and even likes you—which includes all your joys, sorrows, and lamentations.

This book can be a prayer of lament for you and me. It was designed to help us view and experience our daily struggles as God's work of art is still in process. Yet, we must hold on to our hope in Him when it feels like our world's falling apart.

Personal Reflections

Expressions of pain are essential for prayer. Ask yourself these questions: Am I hiding from any kind of pain? Why am I hiding from it? Naming these things might be the perfect starting point for your prayer of lament.

When you read through the Bible the different psalms or prayers of lament, notice the different types of laments: personal grief, corporate suffering, repentance, longing for justice, to name a few. What phases can you relate to personally? Write them in your journal or underline them in your Bible.

Additional Scripture: Psalm 17, Job 13:20–28, Psalm 88

Personal Expressions

While using the suggested steps in this chapter, write your prayer of lament or choose one from the Bible. What image or colors come to your mind? Look through magazines or old books you don't mind tearing pages out of and make a collage of the pictures, words, and colors that express your lamentation.

🔊 **Listen to** *Seasons* **by Hillsong Worship**

Closing Prayer

As the deer longs for streams of water,
so I long for you, O God.
I thirst for You, the living God.
When can I go and stand before You?
Why am I discouraged?
Why is my heart so sad?
O Lord, have compassion on me, for I am weak.
Heal me, Lord, for my bones are in agony.
I am sick at heart.
How long, O Lord, until you restore me?
Return, O Lord, and rescue me.
Save me because of your unfailing love.
Go away, all you who do evil,
for the Lord has heard my weeping.
The Lord has heard my plea;
the Lord will answer my prayer.
I will put my hope in God!
I will praise him again—
my Savior and my God! † **(parts of Psalm 6 and 42)**

CHAPTER 14

Feeling Your Way Through the Dark

Opening Prayer

For my meditation, I am using the Passion of Jesus.
I am afraid I make no meditation,
But only look at Jesus suffer and keep repeating,
Let me share with you this pain!
If my pain and suffering, my darkness and separation,
give you a drop of consolation, my own Jesus,
do with me as you wish.
I am your own.
Imprint on my soul and lift
the suffering of your heart.
If my separation from you brings others to you...
I am willing with all my heart to suffer all that I suffer.
Your happiness is all that I want...
I have begun to love my darkness,
for I believe now that it is a part, a very small part,
of Jesus' darkness and pain on the earth.
I want to satiate Your thirst
with every single drop of blood that You can find in me.
Please do not take the trouble to return soon.
I am ready to wait for You for all eternity. **† Mother Teresa**[1]

---

1   David Scott. "Mother Teresa's Long Dark Night." Chapter 17 in *The Love That Made Mother Teresa*, (Manchester, NH: Sophia Institute Press, 2013) p. 107–113

"Arise, Jerusalem! Let your light shine for all to see.
For the glory of the Lord rises to shine on you.
Darkness as black as night covers all the nations of the earth,
but the glory of the Lord rises and appears over you.
All nations will come to your light;
mighty kings will come to see your radiance. † **Isaiah 60:1–5a**

Story

Even a cloudy night with no moon and stars would be considered light compared to the pitch blackness surrounding me. I pulled my light jacket a little tighter around myself, somehow thinking that would safeguard me from the damp, cold, musty cave air. Because I couldn't see anything, my other senses instinctively worked harder. Somewhere in the dark, I heard a slow and steady drip–drip–drip of water falling into an unseen puddle. In my discomfort, I shifted my weight from one foot to the other, crunching tiny pebbles in the dirt. I stood still, listening to the sound of my own breathing.

Even though this completely dark–dungeon experience lasted only 30 seconds before our family's Grande Cavern tour guide turned his flashlight back on, that feeling of being alone in the dark was all too familiar. But, of course, sometimes, the darkness we experience isn't literal. Occasionally, we experience what feels like darkness while sitting in a staff meeting in the conference room at work, or while you're in a stadium cheering your team, or while cooking dinner for your family, or while standing in church singing worship song from memory and obligation, rather than from the heart.

When struggling in a difficult season, it's as if in your soul, you're in a dark, damp, and cold cave that you've tried to find your way out of but cannot. You're tired of feeling your way around in the dark. Hope can sometimes be hard to find in the dark. You are not the only one who has felt this way. These feelings are not new. Around 875 years before Jesus was born, the prophet Elijah spent time in many dark caves—literally and figuratively speaking.

Elijah was a man God ordained to instruct and encourage the Israelites of His truth and even warn them of their consequences if they continually chose to disobey God. He was a man who faithfully obeyed God and hated evil. And like any of us, Elijah faced discouragement and was tempted to run away from difficult circumstances. While Elijah was spreading the word of God, he repeatedly went up against the evil king Ahab of Israel and told him and his people to turn back to God and stop worshipping Baal, a false god.

In 1 Kings 18:16-45, we read how God did a "showdown" through Elijah against Jezebel, king Ahab's wife, and Baal's 450 prophets. Elijah instructed Baal's prophets to sacrifice a bull and put it on a wooden alter but not set it on fire, and he would do the same.

Elijah told them, "Call on the name of your god, and I will call on the name of the Lord. The god who answers by fire—he is God." (1 King 18:24)

For hours Jezebel's people called out Baal's name, but not even a flicker of fire or puff of smoke emerged from the alter. Finally, Elijah prepared his bull later that day, even pouring buckets of water over the sacrifice and wood. Elijah then prayed to the Lord, asking Him to turn the people's hearts back to Him. When the prayer ended, the sacrifice and wood went up in flames, along with the wet stones and soil underneath it. When Jezebel found out, she became outraged and determined to kill Elijah, knowing she was serious.

That must have been Elijah's last straw. He had been working for God for years and felt like he hadn't made any difference. He thought he was the only one who still believed and worshipped God, and everyone else was out to get him. So naturally, in fear, anxiety, and loneliness, Elijah literally ran for his life to escape being murdered.[2] Elijah struggled. He knew God intimately, yet he felt all alone, abandoned, anxious, and depressed at the same time. Sometimes when we feel alone, we seek a place to be alone, even though that isn't necessarily how we want to be. Elijah did this and left his servant in Judah to journey alone into the mountainous desert. Alone.

For 40 days and 40 nights, Elijah walked 200 miles, isolated from everything and everyone. I vision him walking slowly, almost dragging, with his head down, looking more at the ground and weeds than up at the blue sky painted with white, cumulus clouds. He wasn't wandering aimlessly. He was going to Mount Horeb, where Moses was when God gave him the laws of the people, probably with the hope that God would do another miracle for him there because he felt like he desperately needed one. Finally, by the strength God had given him, Elijah arrived at his destination, and that dark night, went into a cave to sleep.

But the more I thought about Elijah's 40 days and nights journey, I realized that most of those nights were spent in damp, dark caves, alone.

But Elijah wasn't alone. When Elijah was in the cave, the Lord was with him. In the dark. That is the same for us. When we feel alone, more than often, other people are there for us, or who also face the temptation to run and hide; so, you and I are not the only ones.

This reality is shown in Elijah's circumstance when we read 1 King 19:18. After Elijah's 40-day journey to Mount Horeb, the Lord gave him new instructions, and at the end of them, the Lord told Elijah, "Yet I will preserve 7,000 in Israel who have never bowed down to Baal or kissed him!" It seems to me that Elijah had become so despaired that he wasn't aware of the thousands of others who were on his side standing firm in their faith in the one true God and who also had to have struggled with temptations to run and hide from the dominance of unbelievers.

---

2   1 Kings 19:3

Elijah, who never lost his deep commitment to God, still became a victim of the lies he (or the enemy) told him. He fought a cancerous infection of isolation and loneliness that spurred him to say to the Lord, "Take my life, for I am no better than my ancestors who have already died."[3]

It makes us wonder: "How can God be with me when my days feel like dark nights in a cave, when Scripture says, 'God is Light', and in Him, there is no darkness at all?[4] God wouldn't be in a dark cave because his light would shine, right?"

That's what I thought. Until a quiet thought came to my mind, "All birthing and healing begin in the dark."

Seeds are planted deep in the damp, cool, and dark soil under the ground surface. Babies are conceived and grow their first nine months of life in the warmth of a mother's dark womb. When a scratch or wound begins to heal, unseen in a body, new tissue forms from red blood cells creating new skin over the tissue.[5]

And Jesus knows what it's like to experience metaphorical and literal darkness, as well as the dark emotions that come with grief and heartache. On the last night of his life on this earth, before his death, Jesus faced crushing darkness as He prayed to God to save him from what he was about to experience on the cross. The six hours before Jesus died, as he hung on the cross, in the middle of the day, but as He died, the sky became almost as dark as night. After his death, he was buried in the darkness of a tomb—a cave.

Yet. Yet! Once he defeated Satan, the ruler of sin, he resurrected. His body healed, and his heart began to beat again. His lungs filled with air inside a pitch-black cave made into a tomb. In that dark space, a battle waged, but it was also a time of rebirth, healing, and resurrection.

---

3   1 Kings 19:4
4   1 John 1:5
5   Debra Wechter, Debra G. MD, "How Wounds Heal." *Medline Plus,* 8 October 2021, https://medlineplus.gov/ency/patientinstructions/000741.html

And that, friend, is what is taking place in the darkness of our souls. New life is beginning to take shape into something we still cannot see, smell, touch, hear or feel. It's in the depths of darkness where we cannot see. But, just like Elijah, we are not alone in the dark caves of life. It's hard to see in the dark. When we cannot see Him, it's hard to remember that God's presence is with us. Sometimes He is silent, but that doesn't mean He's not there. Even if you cannot see or feel His presence, *know* that He is there doing work deep within that *will* one day give you new life.

Dark seasons in life do not mean that you'll run out of faith, that God has abandoned you, or that you're alone and no one else feels like they're living in a dark cave as you are. Instead, it means that your soul, hidden inside your body, is a secret place where the roots of faith grow deeper. We often equate darkness with scary or haunted places, but it can also be a sacred space where God's unseen and unknown work occurs. In the dark, He prepares us for rebirth and resurrection, so hold onto hope. One day light will break through the darkness like a ray of sun streaming through a crack in a cave or the switch of a flashlight in a tourist cavern.

Personal Reflections

How does it make you feel after reading how Elijah and Jesus struggled through darkness in their lives? How hopeful does it make you feel?

Describe the dark cave season you've been in in the past or currently. How was it different from a season of light and joy? What do you think caused the light to go dim?

Additional Scripture: Mark 14:32-36, Luke 23:44-49, Lamentations 3

Personal Expressions

Create a picture of your cave season. Maybe use some black construction paper and white or colored chalk or chalk pastels (or paint) to add depth. Include a ray or rays of light, if you feel led, to represent the Light of the World in the dark. Or consider how you think you'd see God in the cave with you? How would you be able to know He is there? Then, create a piece of art representing that image.

🔊 **Listen to *Elijah* by Rich Mullins**

Closing Prayer

God, Creator of the heavens and the earth, before You formed light and life, there was darkness, and You were there, and You were good, there in the darkness. Today, I'm tempted to believe that You are no longer present in darkness. I feel like I do not know, nor do I understand; I walk about in darkness as if the earth's foundation is unstable, groping at noontime as if I were in the night. Yet, You made darkness Your secret place. Indeed, the darkness shall not hide from You. So, when I feel trapped in a pit or surrounded by dense, gray fog, please remind me that the darkness and the light are both alike to You—and You are good. Amen. † **(Genesis 1:2, Psalm 82:5, Job 5:14, Psalm 18:11, Psalm 139:12)**

CHAPTER 15

Giving Up on Prayer

Opening Prayer

God, WHERE ARE YOU!? What have I done to make you hide from me? Are you playing cat and mouse with me, or are your purposes larger than my perceptions? I feel alone, lost, forsaken.

You are the God who majors in revealing yourself, You showed yourself to Abraham, Isaac, and Jacob. When Moses wanted to know what you looked like you obliged him. Why them and not me?

I am tired of praying. I am tired of asking. I am tired of waiting. But I will keep on praying and asking and waiting because I have nowhere else to go.

Jesus, you, too, knew the loneliness of the desert and the isolation of the cross. And it is through your forsaken prayer that I speak these words. Amen.

† Richard J Foster *Prayer: Finding the Heart's True*[1]

Rejoice in our confident hope. Be patient in trouble and keep on praying.

† Romans 12:12

---

1 Richard J. Foster. *Prayer: Finding the Heart's True Home*, (San Francisco: Harper, 1992) p. 24-25

Story

Prayer is one of the most powerful actions of faith. It's an intimate way of being in the presence of God. But when you've been praying specifically for something for a long time, and it seems like you're talking to a brick wall, you might begin to question if God is even listening or wonder if He hears you. At least that happened to me.

What have you prayed about that you feel God hasn't answered? A new job? A restored relationship? You and your spouse can start a family? That your baby will start sleeping through the night? A cure for chronic insomnia? A clear answer for a significant decision you must make? What is yours right now?

My prayer was, "Lord, please deliver me from my depression. I know You have the power to do it. If you heal me, I'll be willing and able to do more for You." I prayed that prayer repeatedly for months, which turned into a couple of years. I prayed that prayer silently or aloud while sitting, kneeling, or even laying prostrate on the floor. I wrote that prayer and sang that prayer. Finally, after two years of unanswered prayer, I stopped praying. It felt like God ignored me and didn't care about me anymore.

When I believed that lie, anger emerged. Anger is not an emotion I usually welcome into my mind. If you asked those who know me well, if I easily become angry, they'd say, "No way!" Usually, I brush that emotion off my sleeve, but a small portion of it nestles in the back corner of my soul closet, hidden. Occasionally, anger makes its way to the door, turns the knob, and bursts out. That is rare for me, but when my hidden anger comes out, it explodes (as you read one of those rare cases in *Do You Feel Anxious*).

As I said above, one of the few times I've felt angry at God was when He didn't answer my prayers for relief from depression after praying for healing for a couple of long years. I didn't understand why He allowed me to be stuck in that illness. But, through the years, I've learned that there are different reasons why our prayers are not answered or why they have not been answered the way we want them to be answered. I know there's still much more for God to teach me, but these are some of the reasons for unanswered prayers.

Sometimes we think God isn't answering a specific prayer because the request isn't turning out exactly the way we asked or desired. We can think our way is the best way even though we're trying to control the situation with our preferred outcome. When we're so set on wanting a particular outcome, we can overlook how God *is* answering that prayer—just a different and better way. Often, God shouldn't answer our prayers the way we want them answered because He has a greater purpose and plan.

Or, He was not saying anything *yet* for a specific reason. It is a possibility someone or something needs to happen before your prayer can be answered. Or the Lord isn't answering your request because He wants to meet your eternal needs instead of your temporary or immediate wishes.

There are yet more lessons God has been teaching me about prayer—or giving it up. I've not been able to find anywhere in the Bible God's instructions for us to not pray except for one place in Exodus 14 where God tells His people to stop praying. The rescued Egyptian slaves prayed and prayed and kept waiting for an answer, and God told them to stop praying and get moving because God caused the Red Sea to part in two once they did. That recorded incident is for a different time, though. Every other mention of prayer in the Bible encourages, teaches, or tells us to pray.

Next time you're in a funk, or when you've prayed the same request a million times and still received no answer, I dare you to give up, too. There's a giving-up called quitting, but there's also a giving-up called surrender. There's a difference between quitting and surrendering. Quitting is believing you can no longer continue to do what you've been trying to do, and so you no longer try. Surrendering is when you think you can no longer continue to do something, and you desperately need Jesus to take the reins and reign.

When it comes to prayer, God doesn't want us to get to the point where we quit. When we're at the moment when the temptation to quit comes to our minds, He wants us to surrender instead. We can give up fighting our inabilities or lack of desire to the Lord when the power of the Holy Spirit takes charge and prays for us.

When Paul was writing a letter to the new believers in Rome, part of that letter (specifically Romans 8) gives a powerfully concise and beautifully summarized description of the Gospel and God's entire Story. However, there's one part of chapter eight that pierces straight to our innermost being when we can no longer pray.

In the same way, the Spirit helps us in our weaknesses. We do not know what we ought to pray for, but the Spirit himself intercedes for us through wordless groans. And he who searches our hearts knows the mind of the Spirit because the Spirit intercedes for God's people in accordance with the will of God. (Romans 8:26–27)

God has always known that we were not created to live without Him. He knows there will be times we're broken, shocked, or damaged and no longer can pray. He knows our desires will seem to have vanished. Our hope will fade away. Our trust will die. When we feel that way, our deep longings can become exposed through our emotions mentally and physically, including wordless groans.

The Greek word for "groan" that Paul used when he wrote this letter is *stenazó* which means "compressed, constricted...like the forward pressure of *childbirth*.[2] When you read Romans 8:18-23, Paul writes how all of God's creation has been groaning like the pains of childbirth. Struggling and pain occur before new life in a new heaven and earth after Jesus' second coming. Thankfully, Paul continues to tell us that God has given us the Holy Spirit to intercede for us prayerfully during those pains. Prayer is so vital HE will pray for you. When you're at your lowest, He prays on your behalf. When you surrender your unanswered or wordless prayers and groans, His Spirit is in tune with your soul and offers your prayer to God.

People from every generation have lived through troubling times. There's so much stuff we try to wrap our brains around, and that's the enemy's tactic to keep us distracted from wrapping our minds around Christ. Repeated pain, fear, and rejection can cause us to think we're praying incorrectly, disappointing God, or that God is not with us. But He *is* present. His name, Emmanuel, means "God with us." His Name will never change; therefore, He will be with us always.

He is with us regardless of the "even if's" that come to our minds because of doubt. Even if we desire to pray but can't form words due to our crushed heart and spirit, the Holy Spirit prays for us. And that is not the only *even if.*

Even if we don't hear Him, He hears you and me. He hears us even if all we can do is groan. He hears the longing in our soul that even we cannot hear ourselves. In Psalm 38:9, David writes how he too experienced this: "*All my longings lie open before you, O Lord; my sighing is not hidden from you.*" God hears, understands, and honors our sighs, groans, cries, or silence.

Even if we don't understand, He understands. It is normal to question God about unanswered prayers. We ask God why a situation, or life in general, isn't getting better. We want to know

---

2   *Bible Hub.* "4727. stenazó," 2021, https://biblehub.com/greek/4727.htm

what's happening, why it's happening, and when it's going to stop or start happening. Jesus understands why we feel the way we do, so allow that truth to give you peace and rest by simply being with Emmanuel.

Even if we don't have the words, we can honor God by being in His presence. At the beginning of this chapter, I mentioned a time when I was struggling with my prayers. I sought godly counsel from one of my spiritual directors, Fil Anderson. When I met with him, he told me about his personal experience of struggling with prayer. I was surprised that such a grounded and wise Christ-follower and teacher would have struggled with prayer. But he had. And so, had I.

His tender words of wisdom explained how simply being with the Trinity—God, Jesus, and the Holy Spirit—in solitude, stillness, and silence can be a life-changing experience when it comes to prayer and being present with God. Praying doesn't always involve formed or spoken words. By surrendering our frustrations, doubts, grief, anxiety, depression, and any other obstacle that keeps us from feeling close to God, we are honoring Him.

Another suggestion Fil gave me when it comes to needing help with prayer is to find a book or two of written prayers that you simply read and offer to God as your prayer. This book includes some I've used for the opening prayers. When you're struggling to pray, also try praying Scripture. An example of this is in *The Storms* and the closing prayers of each chapter in this book.

When you can't even do those different prayer forms, ask someone to pray for you. You don't have to be specific and explain details. I have learned that God does not ignore our prayers. Life's ups and downs, God's will, and purposes are not always smooth and easy. Unanswered prayer can make us feel like we're treading water, fighting to stay afloat. But God is still with you and me. He may not be answering your requests yet, but He is present with you, taking you to solid ground.

Personal Reflections

I mentioned a few different ways to pray. One of them is to read a prayer already written. They can be found in hymnals, books about prayer, books of prayers, and of course, the Bible. So take some time to find some written prayers and then make time to be in solitude and read the prayers as an offering to God.

Practice the holiness of solitude and silence. When praying, we're in God's presence. Turn your phone or other devices off or put them in another room. Be attentive. Listen. Hum or sing a hymn or Christian worship song. And don't be surprised if the Holy Spirit gives you words to pray. But maybe He won't, and that's OK.

Additional Scripture: Matthew 6:9–13, 2 Samuel 22, Psalm 38

Personal Expressions

Using crayons or markers, re-write in your personal handwriting a Scripture prayer. Allow it to take a large portion of the space on the paper. You can add doodles around the words. Listen to some worship music or be in silence. May it be a time of worship and prayer when you don't have to say a word.

🔊 **Listen to** *The Lord's Prayer* **by Hillsong Worship**

Closing Prayer

Oh Lord, you have searched me, and you know me. You know when I sit and when I rise, you perceive my thoughts from afar. You discern my going out and my lying down; you are familiar with all my ways. Before a word is on my tongue, you know it completely, Oh Lord. You hem me in—behind and before; you have laid your hand upon me. Such knowledge is too wonderful for me, too lofty for me to attain. Search me, Oh God, and know my heart; test me and know my anxious thoughts. See if there is any offensive way in me and lead me in the way everlasting. Amen † **(Psalm 139)**

CHAPTER 16

Tears

Opening Prayer

Almighty, most Holy, most High God, thank You for paying attention to small things. Thank You for valuing the insignificant. Thank You for being interested in the lilies of the field and the birds of the air. Thank You for caring about me. In Jesus' name.

† Richard Foster *Prayer: Finding the Heart's True Home*[1]

You keep track of all my sorrows.
You have collected all my tears in your bottle.
You have recorded each one in your book. **† Psalm 56:8**

Story

In one hand, my dad tightly gripped his wooden, clinging cross. In his other hand, he held mine. It was hours before he lost his battle to cancer but gained victory in heaven. He was not opening his eyes or speaking anymore, but when he squeezed my hand at different times when I was reminding him of the special memories we had made together, I knew he heard me and had been listening. After I read Romans 8 to him, and after I told him I

---

1   Richard J. Foster. *Prayer: Finding the Heart's True Home* (San Francisco: Harper, 1992) p. 178

loved him again, he squeezed my hand again. I didn't want him to hear me crying, though, as I silently licked the salty tears that rolled down my face.

Many countless tears rolled down my face for the months to come after that August evening. At least countless to me, but not to God. In one of his psalms of lament, David wrote how God keeps track of all our sorrows and collects all our tears, records the number of each one, and puts them in a bottle.[2]

A tangible example of our deep, emotional Savior was in the gospel book of John when Lazarus died. When reading chapters 11 and 12, we learn that Jesus had become close friends with Lazarus, Mary, and Martha. Chapter 11 is the written recording of what happened to Lazarus, Mary's, and Martha's brother, and what happened to Jesus and Lazarus' sisters. Lazarus had become deathly ill and died four days before Jesus got to them. Frustrated and grieved, Mary and Martha did not understand why Jesus did not come sooner.

John describes Jesus' arrival this way,

"When Jesus saw Mary weeping, and the Jews who had come along with her also weeping, he was deeply moved in spirit and troubled. 'Where have you laid him?' he asked. 'Come and see, Lord," they replied. Jesus wept." (John 11:33–35)

You may have heard or read that shortest sentence in the Bible— *Jesus wept.* John chose that strong, descriptive word for a reason. Jesus didn't whimper, sniffle, or shed a few tears—he wept. He sobbed, moaned, or maybe as we sometimes say, cried an ugly cry. So what was it that triggered Jesus to express his soulful emotions?

Many scholars and theologists have written interpretations of Jesus' response to Lazarus' death. Some say he was "angry," while others

---

2 Psalm 56:8

believe it was "furious indignation." The Greek term *embrimáomai* in verses John 11:33 and 38 often translates to "deeply moved." In other places in scripture, that word was used when Jesus "strongly warned" the people he healed not to tell others. Even though these are all slightly different interpretations, they all relate to deep, human emotions that can lead to tears and weeping. John included this rawness of Jesus because many people (then and now) perceive God as a deity without emotions or feelings, especially grief, sorrow, and tenderheartedness. Scripture shows us otherwise. God is compassionate and tender, especially when it comes to our tears.

Tears are an interesting part of our humanness. In an article in Time magazine titled "Science of Tears," the writer explains that scientists can easily prove the existence of a lacrimal gland in our eyes that causes tears to keep the eye moist or cleanse them when an intrusion enters the eye.[3] But, they are still trying to scientifically understand why and how deep emotions, whether joy, grief, or anger, can activate tears to flow. While intricately creating us, God included glands to produce tears and emotions to somehow release through healthy and healing tears.

In Western culture, especially in America, crying is sometimes seen as a weakness. If you feel lost, frustrated, or hurt, we sometimes repress our emotions because we don't want anyone else to know how we truly feel. It's OK to suppress our feelings for a short period, but when we don't allow ourselves to process and pray about our negative emotions, our health is compromised. Tears are powerful. Not weak. Tears are woven into our lamentations when we call out to God for help while expressing our truest feelings.

God honors our tears. Psalm 56 says that He stores each one in a bottle. He treats each one tenderly because our tears are a

---

3   Mandy Oaklander. "The Science of Crying." *Time*, 16 March 2016, https://time.com/4254089/science-crying/

language only the Holy Spirit can speak when our minds don't know how to find the words to explain our souls' longings. "God receives and tenderly holds tears as if they are precious, explosive testimony that must be preserved for some future day. Perhaps this vigilant, seeing, and tear-collecting God weeps with the world."[4]

Brennon Manning, a modern-day Franciscan priest, spiritual director, and author, penned these words in his book *Abba's Child: The Cry of the Heart for Intimate Belonging*

> *"Live in the wisdom of accepted tenderness. Tenderness awakens within the security of knowing someone thoroughly and sincerely likes us."*

He goes on to say,

> *"How would you respond if I asked you this question: 'Do you honestly believe God likes you, not just loves you because theologically God has to love you?' If you could answer with gut-level honesty, 'Oh, yes, my Abba is very fond of me', you would experience serene compassion for yourself that approximates the meaning of tenderness."*[5]

Accept God's tenderness. It's OK to cry. It's actually healthy to cry, and God designed us to express our deepest feelings without words through tears. If you feel them welling up in your eyes, unleash your tears and don't try to hold them back. As each tear brings grief and sorrow out from within, the Holy Spirit can refill your soul's open space with His peace and comfort. I don't think God allows all our grief and sufferings to go away because there's a sacredness in suffering, and tears can be holy water that cleanses our wounded hearts. Let us remember our Father's tenderness for us when we're falling apart.

---

4 Kathleen M. O'Connor. *Lamentations and the Tears of the World*, (New York: Orbis Books, 2002), p. 130

5 Brennan Manning. *Abba's Child: The Cry of the Heart for Intimate Belonging*, (Colorado Springs, CO: NavPress, 1994), p. 46

I don't think the only time Jesus wept while he was on this side of eternity was when Lazarus died—they just weren't recorded. I would not be surprised if many of his prayers to his Father were accompanied by sacred, watery, human tears. Jesus' tenderness is evident in his interactions with his disciples and with the people following him as he talked with them, asked them questions, ate meals with them, sat with them at wells, and healed them. As he listened to their stories, he looked directly into their eyes, which may have included tears. He understood them and empathized with them, just like the Holy Spirit does with us today.

God, our Father, is so fond of you, my friend. He takes you by the hand and invites you to accept His tenderness. Even more, He sympathizes with you—not just send you a Hallmark card, but he *co-suffers* with you, which is the original definition of the word sympathize. He literally feels your grief.

When we accept God's tenderness, we also need to be tender to ourselves. Sometimes it's easy to be hard on ourselves. Check your internal monologue and what you tell yourself. Are they negative comments or tender ones when it comes to your emotions? What kind of self-esteem do you have? Do you feel confident through Christ or give in to the enemy's lies? How harsh are your thoughts about how you look or the decisions you make? Is guilt your companion instead of grace? How much energy do you have? Are you overextending yourself day after day? When we aren't compassionate to ourselves, and when we don't allow tears to release our emotional tension to relieve our souls, then we aren't accepting God's tenderness in our lives.

Live with tenderness. Shed some tears every now and then, and remember that God holds every tear.

That August day, when my dad was holding one of my hands, my Heavenly Father was holding my other, while with His other hand, He held a jar to collect my tears to keep them for a future day when they can be used as a testimony for His goodness and tenderness. And He has one for you, too.

Personal Reflections

Are you one who does not like to show your emotions, especially in the form of tears, or are you one who can cry in the blink of an eye? Consider your own beliefs about tears. Then, in your journal, reflect on your thoughts or beliefs about displaying emotion through tears. Dig deep—where do your beliefs have their roots?

As mentioned above, Brennon Manning instructs people to "live in the wisdom of accepted tenderness." How do you feel about living out that statement?

Additional Scripture: Luke 7:36–50, Philippians 2:1–8, John 11:1–44

Personal Expressions

Find an old glass jar in your home and make a Tear Bottle as a reminder of God's tenderness for you. You can use a craft adhesive such as Mod Podge to adhere different colored tissue paper that you cut into shapes or a drawing you made to adhere to the jar. Possibly include the words of Psalm 56:8 somewhere on the jar. Then put it in a place, even if it's a secret place, that you can see when you're sad, grieving, angry, fearful, or even full of joy, to remind yourself how much God likes you and has a tender heart for you.

🔊 **Listen to** *When I Get to Where I'm Going* **by Brad Paisley**

Closing Prayer

Abba, I am worn out from sobbing. All night I flood my bed with weeping, drenching it with my tears. My vision is blurred by grief; my eyes are worn out because of all my enemies. Day and night, I have only tears for food, while my enemies continually taunt me, saying, "Where is this God of yours?" My heart is breaking. Yet, I call You "Abba Father." For Your, Spirit joins with my spirit to affirm that I am Your child. And since I am your child, I am Your heir. Together, with your Son, Jesus Christ, I am also an heir of Your glory. But I know and am willing to share in Jesus' suffering so I can share in Your glory. I trust and believe that You will wipe away every tear from my eyes, and death shall be no more, neither shall there be mourning, nor crying, nor pain anymore, for the former things will pass away when You return. In Jesus' Name, I pray, Amen. † **(Psalm 6:6–7, Psalm 42:3-4a, Romans 8:15-17, Revelation 21)**

CHAPTER 17

Flames and Ashes

Opening Prayer

My prayer is but a cold affair,
Lord, because my love burns with so small a flame,
but you who are rich in mercy
will not mete out to them (your friends) your gifts
according to the dullness of my zeal,
but as your kindness is above all human love
so let your eagerness to hear
be greater than the feeling in my prayers.
Do this for them and with them, Lord,
so that they may speed according to your will,
and thus ruled and protected by you,
always and everywhere.
May they come at last to glory and eternal rest,
through you who are living and reigning God,
through all ages.

Amen † **St. Anselm (England 1033–1109)**

And yet, O Lord, you are our Father.
We are the clay, and you are the potter.
We all are formed by your hand. † **Isaiah 64:8**

Story

Red, orange, and yellow flames engulfed the Mackintosh building at the Glasgow School of Art in Scotland. The original structure was built in 1909. In 2014, the school caught on fire, damaging the west side of the building. Just days after the building had been restored from that fire, around 11 pm on June 15, 2018, the same building caught fire once again, this time suffering "extensive damage." Beautiful architecture and art now lay in ashes resting on the building's foundation.

After the first fire in 2014, a group of artists came together to make beauty out of ashes. Literally. When the flames stopped roaring, the smoke dissipated, and the ashy puddles of water evaporated, artists who created, studied, and taught at the school, rummaged through the aftermath. They picked out some remnants of burnt historical tables, chairs, art easels, and walls and made them into new art pieces. Most used charcoal ashes as the medium to draw pictures. Many art pieces made from the ashes were sold as a fundraiser for the *Ash to Art Auction,*[1] to raise money to restore the devastated building. When I was scrolling through the different compositions created and sold for this project, one particular piece of art caught my attention. While most of the pieces were black and shades of gray because those are the colors the ashes produce, one called "A Given" was bronze. The artist, Douglas Gordon, had put the burnt wood through a fiery, bronze casting process.

Not only does the distinct color of gold cause me to linger a little longer at this artistry, but also its shape. The burnt wood recovered at the destruction was the form of a cross. A little abstract, yet clear. Gordon described his work as such: "My piece has

[1] Kevin Rawlinson. "'Heartbreaking': Fire Guts Glasgow School of Art for Second Time." *The Guardian,* 16 June 2018, https://www.theguardian.com/uk-news/2018/jun/16/firefighters-tackle-blaze-at-glasgow-school-of-art

a kind of religious, or at least a devotional gesture, to it."[2] I don't know anything about Gordon's thoughts about God, but I agree with the title of this piece of art. You may have heard someone say, "It's a given," implying someone knows it's a fact. Regardless of Gordon's belief, it's a fact, a given, that Gordon saw an image of a cross the same as I did when I looked at the piece on my screen. The shape of the charred wood was a given—a cross.

When first found, the burnt object was black, not wood brown. The cross had no perfect, 90-degree angles at any edges like we are used to seeing in churches and jewelry. The width was not like a two-by-four piece of wood purchased at the hardware store, but instead, different levels emerged after the heat from the fire had taken away the original dimensions of the wood. Nevertheless, this cross can fit in a hand.

The human feelings Jesus experienced were a given, a fact, as well. After being tortured, he carried his large and heavy cross a long distance as the pain-wracked His body. Then, Jesus hung with his hands and feet nailed to the wooden cross. I can only imagine how he felt, burning in pain, suffering from intense loneliness and abandonment, and charred joy.

Jesus cried out in angst. "Why have You turned Your back to me? Why have You allowed this to happen? Why couldn't You choose a different way to do Your plan for me?"

Have you cried out to God with similar questions, if not the same ones? I have. Maybe your questions sound like these:

Why do I feel empty, as if my clay jar has a crack in it and can no longer hold onto the joy I once had? Why do I feel like I'm the only one, and no one else can understand my longing? Why does it feel like my dreams, joy, passions, desires, and longings have gone up in flames, and all that remains are burnt remnants? Why God? Why have you allowed me to feel this way?

---

2 "Ash to Art." *Glasgow School of Art*, 2014, http://ashtoart.org/project

We may not know the answers to these questions any time soon, but when you're struggling from emptiness, grief, or pain, as believers, we can search through the rubble of what feels damaged in our lives and discover remnants we cannot see until we look closer. Trust me. It's a given, an actual fact.

There are several references in the Bible about remnants, especially in the Old Testament when the author describes the aftermath of a battle, war, or the destruction of Israel or another country or tribe the Israelites defeated. Because of Israel's sinful actions and behavior against God's commands, He often allowed the Israelites to be attacked and defeated. Yet, amidst the devastation, a few left standing remained who desired to have a relationship with Him—they were His remnants.

The people who survived may have been injured or abused. They may have become homeless and had all their belongings destroyed. They may have lost friends and family. They were probably worried, scared, grieving, exhausted, and tempted towards hopelessness. Those who remained, God's remnants, felt like their lives had gone up in flames, and now, they had to try to pick up the pieces and move on.

Micah is one of the minor prophets in the Old Testament whom God used to teach the people during his generation about the need to repent from sin and return to God. God hates sin yet loves people. In fact, He loves us so much, He gives us the freedom to choose to welcome His love and love Him back by desiring to obey His instructions and have a relationship with Him or not. When raising children, there are consequences when they don't live within the boundaries they're given. When choices are ignored and intentionally disobeyed, there are consequences.

But Micah describes how the Lord sees the people who tried to live out lives for Him—His remnants:

> "*Someday, O Israel, I will gather you; I will gather the remnant who are left. I will bring you together again like sheep in a pen, like a flock in its pasture.*" † (**Micah 2:12**)

And then a little later wrote:

> *"Those who are weak will survive as a remnant; those who were exiles will become a strong nation. Then I, the Lord, will rule from Jerusalem as their king forever."* † **(Micah 4:7)**

We're God's remnants. The victorious One calls us. The Lord, our Good Shepherd, speaks to us individually and gently, calling us His sheep, which, when lost, are returned to the protected pen of His presence. And from our weakness and dependence on Him, we'll become part of God's strong nation.

You, friend, are still here—a living remnant of our living God. Yes, we will suffer and struggle after other fires in our lives. Sometimes it will be as if all our joy and hope has gone up in flames and fallen back down as ashes. But while we may be fragile, broken, and feel like almost dried-up clay, God, who is our Potter, is reforming us more into His likeness. God's redemption is breathtakingly beautiful in a way we wouldn't have thought beautiful at first. Our lives might look or feel different, and it can be painful, hurtful, or uncomfortable during the process, but God often allows our struggles to change us to be more like Jesus, like an exquisite piece of art. And that, my friend, is a given, given by the blood and sacrifice of Jesus on the cross.

May you be a faithful remnant, seeing the charring times in your life as an opportunity for God to reshape you to be more like Him.

Personal Reflections

Has there been, or is there currently, a situation in your life that has "gone up in flames" that has left you feeling like you're in some type of exile or like a lost sheep or broken-down soul not knowing what to do next? If so, describe what it is. Or is there a person close to you who's dealing with something you feel you can share this story to encourage them?

Look around your home and see if you have an old clay flowerpot that might be broken or chipped or a dish in the kitchen or dining room cabinet—something that's a remnant and not in its original form. Carefully hold the piece, feel its weight, and look at the crack or missing part as something unique and beautiful. While you hold it, pray to Jesus, your Good Shepherd, thanking Him for protecting you and ask Him to guide and direct you as you become more like Him.

Additional Scripture: Isaiah 28:5, Haggai 1:12–14, Psalm 23

Personal Expressions

Let's create an artistic, abstract cross. Gather some glue and several pieces of construction paper or a brown paper grocery bag (or any paper thicker than typing paper). Decide the size you'd like your cross to be (the size of your hand, for example) and then tear (not cut with scissors), various sizes of rectangles (2–3" in width and 6–12" in length) to form layers and show depth for the vertical part of the cross. Glue each rectangle strip on top of the other until you get it to the thickness you desire. Do the same steps to make the horizontal part of the cross. If you'd like, put color on the cross or words to remind you how you are one of God's remnants whom He wants to protect in His flock and pen.

🔊 **Listen to *I Will Trust You* by Lauren Daigle**

Closing Prayer

Lord, You are my Good Shepherd, and I have all that I need. Your rod and your staff protect and comfort me. You promise me in Your Word that when I go through deep waters, You will be with me, and when I walk through the fire of oppression, I will not be burned up; the flames will not consume me. Instead, as Your Word says, You will reach out Your hand a second time to make a highway and bring back the remnant of Your people. You will gather together the remnant of Your flock of sheep, Your people, and bring them back to Your sheepfold, care for me so I will not be afraid, and make me fruitful. Surely Your goodness and unfailing love will pursue me all the days of my life. Amen.

CHAPTER 18

Why, Lord?

Opening Prayer

Dear Lord, today I thought of the words of Vincent Van Gogh: "It is true there is an ebb and flow, but the sea remains the sea." You are the sea. Although I experience many ups and downs in my emotions and often feel great shifts and clangs in my inner life, You remain the same. Your sameness is not the sameness of a rock, but the sameness of a faithful lover. Out of Your love, I came to life; by Your love, I am sustained, and to Your love, I am always called back. There are days of sadness and days of joy; there are feelings of guilt and feelings of gratitude; there are moments of failure and moments of success; but all of them are embraced by Your unwavering love.

My only real temptation is to doubt Your love, to think of myself as beyond the reach of Your love, to remove myself from the healing radiance of your love. To do these things is to move into the darkness of despair.

Oh Lord, Sea of Love and goodness, let me not fear too much, the storms and winds of my daily life and let me know that there is ebb and flow but that the Sea remains the Sea. Amen. † **Henri Nouwen "Ebb & Flow" in** *The HarperCollins Book of Prayers*[1]

---

1   Henri Nouwen. "Ebb & Flow," in *The HarperCollins Book of Prayers,* comp. by Robert Van de Weyer (New York: HarperCollins Publishers, 1993), p. 274

After Lot had gone, the Lord said to Abram, "Look as far as you can see in every direction—north and south, east and west. I am giving all this land, as far as you can see, to you and your descendants as a permanent possession. And I will give you so many descendants that, like the dust of the earth, they cannot be counted! Go and walk through the land in every direction, for I am giving it to you. † **Genesis 13:14-17**

Story

It's OK to be sad. But why, you may ask.

It's actually healthy. If you try to ignore your feelings of sadness, unhealthy habits begin to form, which only fan the flame of negative emotions and actions.

It's OK to be in the dark.

It's actually normal. Doesn't each day have hours of darkness just like you experience cycles of internal darkness?

In the beginning, there was darkness until God created light, yet He did not eliminate darkness because we need darkness.

Whenever we're in a season of darkness, we try to ignore it, get out of it, or turn on every artificial light there is to avoid it.

Times in the dark, though, can be just as (if not more) essential to our well-being. Darkness can be an opportunity to become more intimate with the God who is omnipresent—He is everywhere.

In the Bible, one person who knew about darkness was Abraham. Back in Genesis, he spent many hours in the dark—physically (before there was electricity) and emotionally and spiritually. Abraham was one of the first who desired to be obedient to God. However, he learned it was not always easy, not even after God called Abraham to follow Him, promising him descendants outnumbering the stars. After that calling, Abraham lived through a famine (Gen. 12:10). Sarai, his wife, had been barren their entire marriage, and they were already in their late 70's (Gen. 13:16).

Additionally, Abraham experienced conflict with his nephew, Lot, and had to fight in a war for 14 years. Finally, Abraham knew what it was like when daytime might as well have been night because, for more than 25 years, Abraham experienced great darkness.

I imagine Abraham lying on a large rock near a cave after the battles have stopped, and people have fallen asleep after the sun disappeared and the coolness of the night settles around him. I imagine stars freckling the black sky, just like Vincent Van Gogh's painting, *A Starry Night*.

Abraham prays, "Why, Lord? Why can't Sarai, my wife, become pregnant? You promised me that I'd have as many descendants as the number of stars I'm looking at right now. You said more than I could even begin to count. I don't understand. Along with that, Lot has turned his back on You and me, and I live every day with war taking place around me, making me, an older man—weary and wondering. Yet, I will still trust You'll keep Your promise. It's the only hope I have to hold onto."

Every night Abraham looked up at the stars, waiting, dark, starry night, after dark, starry night. Like you and me, he was tempted to take control of his troubles to try to fix them himself instead of surrendering them to God. Darkness can cause fear, and the fear of dark nights in our souls can entice us to question our faith and God. The fact that we are human and not deity means that it is natural for us to question God and encounter sadness. What was significant about Abraham is that he didn't give up his hope in the promise God had given him.

When I think about Abraham longing and looking up into the dark, starry night, my mind wanders over to the well-known artist Vincent Van Gogh.

I think Van Gogh probably could relate to Abraham. Not because God had told Van Gogh that he'd have countless descendants, but because both questioned God in the dark days of their lives.

Van Gogh's father was a Dutch Protestant pastor, and Van Gogh followed in his father's footsteps, also going into ministry. For several years, he was a missionary in the slums of London and the coal mines in Belgium. But his unliked, physical appearance and preaching style was rejected by those he ministered to, which pulled him into depression.

His outlet became painting. Little did he know how powerfully God would minister to others through his art. Van Gogh's paintings, such as *The Good Samaritan*, *The Raising of Lazarus*, *The Sower*, and *The Sheaf Binder*, all pointed to Christ. Van Gogh's emotionally reflective paintings were a new concept in art history. He was not ashamed to express his struggles with depression, rejection, and sadness. The juxtaposition of his vibrant paintings along with his works reflecting the Word of God, the truth about evil, and the majesty of God's creation in nature give us a glimpse into what it looked like for him to suffer days of darkness and express it through art.

One of Van Gogh's most known paintings is *The Starry Night*. When I gaze at it for a while, I'm drawn to think of the many times Abraham looked up into the starry night with the same range of emotions and how over 2,000 years later, Jesus looked up into the same starry night. Now, another 2,000 years later, you and I look up into the exact, same starry night, asking God questions.

In the gospels, we read how Jesus would seclude himself to go pray in the dark hours of the morning.

"Very early in the morning, while it was still dark, Jesus got up, left the house, and went off to a solitary place, where he prayed.[2]

He could look up into the heavens and cry out to his Father as he suffered from rejection, weariness, and despair in broad daylight. Jesus experienced what it feels like to live in the darkness in different times of his life.

---

2   Mark 1:35

Van Gogh's favorite color was yellow[3], representing light. Who is the Light? —Jesus is the Light of the world; Jesus is the Light that even the darkness cannot overcome. Even though there are times in your life when you will or have already experienced doubt and darkness, there are still pinpoints of light in the night sky. Those pinpoints of light promise that God, who created the universes, planets, and stars, does not break His promises of eternal life with Him. Life with God will not be all sunny. But even on the dark days, He is present with you. He is present in the light AND the dark. That is His promise, and He is our hope.

Friend, the next time you step out into the black of night, look up at the stars. Each one is a covenant God has kept with Abraham, Jesus, Van Gogh, and you. Then take note of how every single star is surrounded by darkness. The reason you're able to see the stars is that the light of the sun is shining on them. The Light of the Son of God shines on you in the darkness, too. You are a reflection of Jesus, even if you feel like you're in the black void of night. His light shines from you—you don't have to turn on artificial lights to appear bright. All you need to do is be you, and know that God, your Father, loves you. Ask God your questions while in darkness. He wants you to bring your feelings and thoughts to Him. Consider each star you see as a glimmer of hope.

---

3 *Art Through the Ages: II Renaissance and Modern Art.* Horst De La Croix, Richard G. Tansey, Diane Kirkpatrick University of Michigan, Ann Arbor (Harcourt Brace Jovanovich, Publishers Ninth Edition 1991), p. 935

Personal Reflections

Currently, are your days bright and sunny, or do they feel more like night—like darkness, in the daytime? Or are you in a season like Abraham, where you know God has promises for you, but you struggle believing them? What is causing you to feel that way? Ask God to show you how He still keeps His promises.

Go outside on a clear night and look up at the stars. If you're near a location with sand (a beach, lake, sandbox), grab a handful of sand. Now try to count the stars or grains of sand. Think about how much God loves you and has more promises for you than you can count.

Additional Scripture: Genesis 1:1–5, John 1:1–5, Amos 5:8

Personal Reflections

Take some time and find pictures in a book or online of Vincent Van Gogh's paintings *The Good Samaritan*, *The Raising of Lazarus*, *The Sower*, *The Sheaf Binder*, and *A Starry Night*. How do they point to Christ? Which one are you drawn to the most? Why? If you feel up for the experience, find a painting class on YouTube on how to paint one of Van Gogh's pieces of art mentioned above. I did that for *A Starry Night*, and my soul was filled. It won't look exactly like Van Gogh's, but it's not supposed to. It's an act of worship. As you paint, listen to worship music, reflect on the promises of God that He kept with Abraham and you in your life.

🔊 **Listen to *So Will I* by Hillsong Worship**

Closing Prayer

Lord, I will exalt You, for You rescued me. I cried to You for help, and You restored me; You brought me up from the grave. I praise Your holy name! For Your anger lasts only a moment, but Your favor lasts a lifetime! Weeping may last through the night, but joy comes with the morning. Your favor, O Lord, made me as secure as a mountain. Hear me, Lord, and have mercy on me. Help me, O Lord. You have turned my mourning into joyful dancing. You have taken away my clothes of mourning and clothed me with joy, that I might sing praises to You and not be silent. You shake the earth from its place, and its foundations tremble. If You command it, the sun won't rise, and the stars won't shine. You alone have spread out the heavens and marches on the waves of the sea. You made all the stars and constellations and did great things too marvelous to understand. O Lord my God, I will give You thanks forever! Amen.

† (Psalm 30, Job 9:7-10)

CHAPTER 19

Small Faith

Opening Prayer

"God, I cannot thank You enough for the way You have begun to deliver me from my trial. You know very well what I need and that all You do is for my good. The difficulties of life do not have to be unbearable. It is the way I look at them—through faith or unbelief—that makes them seem so. I must be confident that You are full of love for me and that You only permit trials to come my way for my own good. Lord, I want to look to You with the eyes of faith. Amen."

† **Brother Lawrence** *The Practice of the Presence of God*[1]

Deep calls to deep
in the roar of your waterfalls;
all your waves and breakers
have swept over me.

By day the Lord directs his love,
at night his song is with me—
a prayer to the God of my life. † **Psalm 42:7 (NIV)**

---

1 Brother Lawrence Fleming. *The Practice of the Presence of God*, reprint of 1895 edition

Story

Until a few years ago, I could not have said I'd stood in the middle of a rainbow—one that unexpectantly appeared out of the blue, with no sign of a summer thunderstorm around.

Our family left the east coast for a couple of weeks and flew out west to Arizona and California. Our summer vacation included the beginning process of college visits with our daughter. If this so far-away school in Arizona is where she decided to attend, it made this mama feel better knowing that my husband's relatives live 30 minutes from campus.

After the tour and spending a few enjoyable days with family, we repacked, got in the rental car, and headed to the west coast. Finally, we reached Hollywood, California, and Malibu got on highway US-1, and drove north along the Pacific coastline, stopping along the way to spend some time in Monterey, San Francisco, and our final stop, the Yosemite National Park.

None of us had been to Yosemite, and I had wanted to see it in person ever since I admired Albert Bierstadt's painting of it at the art museum in my younger years. We were all amazed at the majestic beauty of the breathtaking views of waterfalls, enormous granite mountains, meadows, wildflowers, and trees that surrounded us in the valley. We were also blessed to be there in the early summer because we could see several massive waterfalls. When the snow on top of the granite mountains melts, the water cascades down its sides, which only lasts for a couple of months.

On our first afternoon there, we hiked on one of the trails to get a closer view of a waterfall. Even from a distance, we saw bright sparkles of sunlight dancing on the water as it rushed down the side of the massive granite shelf. From one-fourth of a mile away, we felt the occasional mist from the waterfall on our faces and arms as we walked on a wooded trail. The sound of rushing water grew louder as we hiked over rocks to get a closer view. Then, when the wind slightly picked up speed, we felt the power of that frigid water cascading down the stone wall.

We passed many people who had been to the end of the trail and returning to the starting point. They had smiles on their faces. The mist became like sprinkling rain when we arrived at the end of the trail. We were close to the cascading water crashing into the massive river that ran down alongside the mountain base. We had only stood there for about thirty seconds, and suddenly, it felt like the sky opened, and it poured rain—thoroughly soaking us! Our daughter was the only one who didn't get soaked, and she happened to get a picture of me at the tail end of the windy, water gust. She wasn't taking a picture of me getting wet, though; she was taking a picture of the rainbow that had just appeared. I had no inkling there was a rainbow until she called out, "Mom! You've got to see this picture! You're standing in the middle of a rainbow!"

Gifted and well-known photographer Ansel Adams once said, "Sometimes I do get to places just when God's ready to have somebody click the shutter."[2]

Standing in the middle of that rainbow, God reminded me that they represent His promise to us. God's covenant to Noah (and all of us) after 40 days and nights of solid rain and flooding is that He will never flood the earth like that again. A covenant is an entirely devoted and deep-down promise given to someone.

Lying in the dark hotel room that night, I revisited earlier that day in my mind—the vastness of God's masterpiece in Yosemite and a rainbow reaching through me. It was refreshing because that was nearing the end of a personal "dark night of the soul"[3] season in my life. In the darkness and silence of that night and season, I heard God whisper to me:

---

2 "Ansel Adams Quotes." BrainyQuote.com. BrainyMedia Inc, 2021. 24 October 2021. https://www.brainyquote.com/quotes/ansel_adams_107190
3 St. John of the Cross. *The Dark Night* between 1577 and 1579

"You were at that waterfall today because I wanted you to notice yourself in a rainbow. Rainbows represent covenants or promises. So I put that rainbow right *through* you to remind you, my beloved, that I AM yours and you are Mine. I've promised that I'm always with you, I uphold you, I counsel you, and give you wisdom and hope. And a rainbow is to remind you that after a storm (in your life) *is* a new start. A new beginning. Something beautiful. And I keep my promises."

Those quiet, comforting words helped me fall to sleep.

In the book of Psalms, we read David's words in chapter 42, where he proclaims how *deep calls to deep in the roar of God's waterfalls.* When we reflect on this psalm, we read an expressive song of lament, where David is crying out to the Lord. The King James Version is a lament of art.

> "As the deer pants for the water brooks, so pants my soul for You, O God. When shall I come and appear before God? My tears have been my food day and night, while they continually say to me, 'Where is your God?' When I remember these things, I pour out my soul within me. Why are you cast down, O my soul? And why are you disquieted within me? Hope in God, for I shall yet praise Him for the help of His countenance. O my God, my soul is cast down within me…deep calls unto deep at the noise of Your waterfalls; all Your waves and billows have gone over me."[4]

Maybe you're like David, and your soul feels dried up and beginning to crack or the opposite where gushing water threatens to take you down. Your appetite is gone, and your anxiety has manifested. Your heart and soul are disquieted—lacking peace. So then, as David describes, *deep calls unto deep.*

What does David mean here? I see it this way. The deep crevasses within our soul call out, expressing deep affliction and grief. Our outward, or physical, turmoil feels deep, causing us to feel

4   Psalm 42 KJV

disturbed, yet the deep, inward depth of God's love and tenderness also resides in our soul and has more power to overcome the distress. Our deep longings cry out in the language only our soul speaks, which only the Holy Spirit can interpret. Honestly, that feeling can be confusing and hard to understand. Yet, here is where we experience our mustard-seed faith in action. There are times in our lives when the water flows from our eyes like a gushing waterfall because internally, the roar of the rushing emotions is so loud. Yet, through God's Word, the Holy Spirit, and by faith, we're given the power to overcome the force of the mighty waves that try to take us down.

Your faith may feel small like a mustard seed, but it's stronger than you know. Do you know about the time when Jesus healed the boy who had epilepsy, along with demons who often threw him in water or fire? Jesus healed him because his disciples had tried but not succeeded. Jesus was correcting his disciples, basically saying they had no faith and had been trying to heal the boy on their own, not through God's power. Jesus says that "if you have faith as small as a mustard seed, you can say to this mountain, 'Move from here to there and it will move. Nothing is impossible for you." (Matthew 17:20)

A mustard seed is tiny, about one to two millimeters in diameter.[5] What is so tiny that begins in the damp and dark soil begins to sprout as nature gently tends to its needs with water and sun that ignites what was once a minute seed to grow into a tree. Our faith is like that mustard seed. So small faith grows to overcome the deep grief and suffering we experience. It's those deep, underground days in our lives where tears and God's tenderness moisten the hardened soul, along with less than a millimeter of your faith.

When we face trials, we may not realize it, but it's the opportunity

---

5   Wikipedia contributors "Mustard Seed" In *Wikipedia, The Free Encyclopedia*
    Retrieved May 1, 2021, from https://en.wikipedia.org/wiki/Mustard_seed

for our faith to deepen. When our faithfulness deepens, we have the power to do things we didn't think were possible. I don't think God usually gives us faith if we don't want it or we don't ask Him for it.

If we want relief in our struggling, we must have the desire for faith so it can grow. Even though we may not be able to understand the turmoil we're experiencing at the moment, have faith in the steadfastness and firmness of God's compassion and affection for you. That is a promise. Sometimes we forget that we have spiritual amnesia where Christians easily forget the extraordinary things God can do.[6] So, friend, here's a reminder, one to try not to forget. When you're in deep waters, remember the deepness of God's tender kindness and love for you. We may be soaked from tears and chilled from darkness, but Jesus is waiting for us beside a warm fire on the beach when we least expect it. Full of grace, full of truth, full of faithful promises. Nothing is impossible with faith in Christ, whether small or big. He can even form a rainbow around us. I promise.

Personal Reflections

In your own words, describe what David meant when he wrote: "Deep calls unto deep."

Do you feel your faith in Jesus is the size of a mustard seed in the dark ground, a sapling emerging from the soil, a growing tree, or a mature tree? Why? How can you tend to your faith to help it grow even more?

Additional Scripture: Mark 4:30–32, Psalm 42, John 21:1–14

---

6   Alan Wright. *The God Moment Principle.* (*Sisters, Oregon,* The Doubleday Religious Publishing Group 2001) p. 41

Personal Expressions

Here are a couple of options for your personal expression with this chapter. 1) If you live near a nursery or a store that sells mustard seeds, purchase one pack and plant one in a pot of fertilized soil, the appropriate amount of water and sunshine. (You might need to transfer it to the ground somewhere!) Or, 2) Create an image, such as a waterfall and/or rainbow, in your journal. You can use markers, crayons, pastels, paint, torn pieces of construction paper—whatever you have on hand. Then, somewhere on the page, include these words: "Deep calls unto deep." While creating it, remember that when you're in deep turmoil, the Holy Spirit is deepening your faith by giving you the power you need to overcome your trial.

🔊 **Listen to *My Redeemer Lives* by Nicole Mullen**

Closing Prayer

Lord, You tell me that faith shows the reality of what I hope for; it is the evidence of things I cannot see. And it is impossible to please You without faith. Anyone who wants to come to You must believe that You exist and that You reward those who sincerely seek You. I cry out to You, Lord, "deep unto deep" when it feels like a waterfall is crashing down on me. But I still praise You, Lord, for Your promises. Your ways are perfect. All Your promises prove true. You are a shield for all who look to You for protection. I praise You, God, for what You have promised; yes, I praise You, Lord, for what You have promised. Amen.

† (Hebrews 11:1, 6; Psalm 18:30; Psalm 56:10)

CHAPTER 20

It's Time to Return to Me

Opening Prayer

Our Father and our God, have mercy on me, a sinner. I truly want to do what is right and good in Your eyes, but evil is always there with me. I am weak and sinful, O Lord. Yet I thank You for Jesus, who will deliver us in triumph over sin, the devil, and evil. Thank You for the cross, which reconciles me to You through Jesus, in whose name I pray. Amen.

† Billy Graham *Unto The Hills: A Daily Devotional*[1]

I am the Lord, and I do not change. That is why you descendants of Jacob are not already destroyed. Ever since the days of your ancestors, you have scorned my decrees and failed to obey them. Now return to me, and I will return to you," says the Lord of Heaven's Armies.

† Malachi 3:6-7

Story

Your heart pounded hard. The butterflies in your stomach wouldn't stop fluttering. Taking a deep breath—well, that just seemed

---

1 Billy Graham. *Unto The Hills: A Daily Devotional*, (New York: Thomas Nelson, 2010) September 14

impossible because all you could take were several short ones. Time seems to drag on when you want to be with the first love of your life again, even if it was just yesterday when you were together.

This first love of yours could have been a new puppy added to your life, or when you were in third grade and had a crush on one of your classmates, or it could have been that love-at-first-sight blind date you went on in college and then before long, wedding bells were ringing. Whenever and whoever your first love was, I'm sure you can remember those giddy feelings.

What about your relationship with God? Maybe there's been a time when you knew and understood how much God truly loves you and wants to spend time with you? Do you recall how that realization led you to invite Him into your heart and mind? Did it feel like a flame ignited? You spent your free time in prayer, reading devotions, and reading non-fiction books by Christian authors. You joined a Bible study and made attending church a priority on the weekend. The worship was authentic, the pastor's teachings were precisely what you needed to hear.

Then after months and years went on, those first love feelings that got you out of bed every day seemed to turn into a routine without much meaning. Of course, you still go through the motions—when you make time or want to. But, those exciting feelings and dedicated, spiritual practices seem to have been thrown into the pile of "to-dos" that seldom got done.

Instead of waking up early to be in the Word, you'd hit the snooze button again. Instead of making your weekly community group or Bible study meeting a priority, your long day at work became a good enough excuse not to go. Instead of making time for prayer, watching another episode on Netflix seems more fun. Sleeping in on Sunday and watching the service online instead of going to church becomes a shallow ritual with little-to-non-experience of worship.

Once that happens, we become more prone to give in to the temptations the enemy dangles in front of our faces. We sin every day because we are human, but when we no longer feel close to the Lord, like we did when we first gave our lives to Him, sin looks, tastes, sounds, feels, and smells better each day. When we allow sin to take control of our decisions, God's heart is bruised because He is a jealous God and wants us to choose Him instead of sin.

This struggle is nothing new. We know that this has been happening since the beginning of time. The Bible is full of stories like ours, stories of love lost, and choices that lead us into temptation. Joel is one of the minor prophets in the Old Testament who has a short, four-chapter book in the Bible; that is not to say, fewer words do not have the power to change us. But, like the other minor prophets, Joel felt led by God to preach the Truth about salvation and how it only happens when people turn away from the sin of worshipping other idols and turn back toward God. Then, God will show them mercy, compassion, and favor when they do.

That stays the same for us, as well. God is the same yesterday, today, and in the future.[2] So, when Joel wrote these words God told him to proclaim, they apply to us today, too.

> "'Even now', declares the Lord, 'return to Me with all your heart, with fasting and weeping and mourning.' Rend (tear) your heart and not your garments. Return to the Lord your God, for He is gracious and compassionate, slow to anger and abounding in love, and he relents from sending calamity. Who knows? He may turn and relent and leave behind a blessing—grain offering and drink offerings for the Lord your God." **(Joel 2:12-14)**

God was telling the people (ahem, *us*) to *return* to *Him* because they had gone their own way by disobeying and turning away from Him again.

---

2   Hebrews 13:8

Return to God with *all* your heart.

God is telling us to return to Him. We do this through confession, repentance, and surrender, sometimes accompanied by tears.

Joel tells the people that God can and will relent—soften His feeling of disappointment—and become compassionate and even forgiving. God, by no means, is mild when it comes to His power—but in His grace and mercy, He's more than willing to forgive and heal our hearts when we recognize the errors of our ways and turn back to Him.

It is not necessarily a sin to be frustrated with God, but what we do in our frustration might be. When we're struggling with sin or difficult circumstances, it can be easy to keep on walking the opposite way of The Way when God doesn't seem to be near.

Return to God, Joel tells us.

God says, "Even now when you're struggling with sin. Even now when your pride is trying to take control. Even now, when your heart is bitter towards someone. Even now, when you're not trusting Me. Even now, when you're blaming everyone or everything for your sin and not owning up to it yourself, return to Me."

Daily.

Jesus even prays for his disciples as we read Luke's gospel in chapter 22. When Jesus was having his last supper with his disciples before his arrest, he made sure to tell Peter (Simon) that he had been praying for him. Jesus knew Peter would betray him in just a few hours as people shouted, "Crucify him!" Peter had walked on water with Jesus. He had been with Jesus's transfiguration on the mountaintop with Moses and Elijah. And, he was one of Jesus's closest disciples, who was going to turn his back to Jesus and look the other way as if he didn't know him.

"Simon, Simon, Satan has asked to sift you as wheat. But I have prayed for you, Simon, that your faith may not fail. And when you have turned back, strengthen your brothers." (Luke 22:31–32)

Beth, Beth, Satan has asked to sift you as wheat. But I have prayed for you, Beth, that your faith may not fail. And when you have turned back, strengthen your brothers and sisters.

There have been plenty of days when I've felt the shame of sin. There have been plenty of days where it's felt like Satan's sifted my heart and soul like wheat and blown it away out into the darkness. But I'm choosing to continue reading and believing that my Savior has prayed for me and that the faith I do have will not fail because of what Jesus did for me on the cross. Even in the thick of suffering, struggling, or sin, Jesus still believes in us. Notice, he doesn't say, "And IF you turn back," but instead, he says, "And WHEN you have turned back."[3]

"*And WHEN you have turned back.*" God believes in our faith in Him. He believes our faith will not fail, and He does not doubt us. God trusts us to do what needs to be done for His Kingdom and glory even though He doesn't *need* us to do His work for Him. He displays His love for us by allowing us to see how He lives in us, works through us, and transforms us to be more like His Son, Jesus, day after day. God does not give up on us and does not turn His back on us, even though we've turned our backs on Him one too many times. Yet, He always wants us to return to Him with a contrite heart so we can feel the love He has for us.

Let's remind ourselves often that God is Who He says He is— "gracious and compassionate, slow to anger and abounding in love."[4] We need to because we need Jesus. It is a never-ending practice that should become a rhythm in our lives.

Daily—return to God, repent, forgive, be compassionate, don't anger easily, abound with love. And when you mess up or are fed up, start over again. Each day is a new beginning, a fresh, merciful start, a blank canvas. Each day God wants us to want Him like two people in love for the first time do.

---

3   John Piper. "He Will Cause Us to Return." *Desiring God,* 14 November 2008, https://www.desiringgod.org/articles/he-will-cause-us-to-return
4   Psalm 103:8 NIV

Personal Reflections

Reflect on what your relationship was like in the early days, months, or years of your faith in Jesus. Has it changed since then? Do you feel separated from or not as close to God as you first became a Christ-follower, or do you feel an even deeper connection with God? Why do you think so?

If you struggle with sin, pray—confess your sin—and repent. Then, give yourself another chance because God is gracious and compassionate and even forgiving when we confess and repent—make a 180-degree turn, turning back to Him.

Additional Scripture: Malachi 3:6–7, Hosea 14, Acts 3:18–26

Personal Expressions

Get a piece of paper and something with which to write or doodle. Listen to *Holy Water* a second time, and while you listen to the lyrics, write the word(s) that are the loudest to your soul. If you feel creative, take one or two of those words, and enlarge them on paper. Decorate the letters or write other words of God's righteousness and love for you inside or around the letters of the word you choose. Enjoy the process and time to doodle.

🔊 **Listen to *Holy Water* by We the Kingdom**

Closing Prayer

Compassionate God, Who is slow to anger and abounding in love, I come before You to confess my sins because I know you are faithful and just to forgive me. Lord, I confess my sins (fill in your confession). I am deeply sorry for what I have done. The sacrifice You desire is a broken spirit. You will not reject a broken and repentant heart, O God. May the words of my mouth and the meditation of my heart be pleasing to you, O Lord, my rock and my redeemer. Amen.

† **(Psalm 103:8, 1 John 1:9, Psalm 38:8, Psalm 51:17, Psalm 19:14)**

PART FOUR

Relief, Perspective, and Viewpoint

CHAPTER 21

Pray Anyway

Opening Prayer

Lord, I trust in Your Word, which assures me, that You are my Rock, my Fortress, my Deliverer, my Shield, my Stronghold, and my Strength in whom I trust. Amen. † **Stormie Omartian**[1]

Each one will be like a shelter from the wind
  and a refuge from the storm,
like streams of water in the desert
  and the shadow of a great rock in a parched land. † **Isaiah 32:2**

Story

It was a mid-March afternoon in Burlington, NC, where I live—the beginning of spring shower season, or should I say storm season? When I heard the meteorologist on our local news channel name the street parallel to ours by a few hundred yards, saying to seek a safe shelter quickly because a tornado is heading our way, we did what he said. My daughter and I huddled together in the laundry room as I held my Bible open to Psalm 23. While praying that psalm, I began to hear a sound I had never heard

---

1 Christianbook. 2021, www.christianbook.com/praying-you-stormie-omartian-cards-box/pd/630255

before. It was as if it was constantly thundering for about three minutes—or maybe like a train heading towards our house.

The lights flickered. We heard from the meteorologist on the TV in the other room say that the possible tornado had moved north of where we lived. We exhaled a sigh of relief, grateful for that breath the good Lord gave us.

Not long after that, some of our friends who live a few miles away from us texted a picture they snapped of their backyard. I could hardly recognize it. None of the trees that once stood tall in their yard were no longing standing. Trash and debris covered the yard and tangled in the neighbors' still standing trees. Siding and shingles from their and neighbors' homes were scattered everywhere in the view.

The next day the National Weather Service declared that an EF–1 tornado with 100 mph wind had touched down in our friends' backyard. It was a miracle our friends were not injured or anyone else in our town. There were predictions the day before that a strong line of storms would come through the state, bringing cooler weather. Earlier in the week, they forecasted a high risk of severe storms. The morning of the tornado, though, was down-graded to a slight chance, so we didn't expect it.

That was not the only storm I experienced that week. Just two days earlier, another storm showed up unexpectantly that had no physical damage, but a painful feeling struck like lightning. It appeared out of the blue, causing my heart to feel ripped open and scattered in a pile around my feet. That surprising storm came in the form of words—in just one sentence—that were spoken directly to me, about me, by someone I knew. Like our friends who lived on the street where the tornado had raced through, I was shocked.

The day after the actual tornado occurred, I felt raw from both of the storms I experienced. On my phone, I have a Bible app that gives daily Scripture. On my way to work, at a stoplight, I had the thought to look at my phone, to read that day's verse, but for some reason, it was as if a little voice inside my head said, *wait until you get to work.* When I pulled into the parking space at work, I learned why I needed to wait until I got there. It started with a few teardrops, but tears fell like pouring rain in seconds. God knew it would make me cry, and that would have been a little dangerous for me to be driving and crying.

The verse I read on my screen was my life verse. But, God knew I needed to read it—again. So, looking at my screen in the car, I read this promise in Romans 15: 13:

> *"I pray that God, the source of all hope, will fill you completely with joy and peace because you trust him. Then you will over-flow with confident hope through the power of the Holy Spirit."*

Later that afternoon, when I got home from my part-time job, I went to our sunroom, my quiet and holy place, to pray. God met me there; He was waiting.

My emotions poured out in prayer like the heavy rain had fallen the day before about the wounding, yet unintentionally hurtful words said to me. God reminded me that He alone is my One Audience. I continued to pray, confessing my own sins and faults and declaring how compassionate He is. Once again, His Spirit proved His love by bringing my soul to rest in the Truth of His Word. The same verse He gave me earlier that morning,

> *"I pray that God, the source of all hope, will fill you completely with joy and peace because you trust him. Then you will over-flow with confident hope through the power of the Holy Spirit."*

The kindness of Jesus, my Lord, said to me, "Beth, I pray that My Father, the Source of all hope, will fill you completely with joy and peace because you trust Me. Then you will overflow with confident hope through My power."

And then, it's as if the Holy Spirit nudged me to read that verse, again and again, phrase by phrase, as a prayer and a form of worship. My soul felt refreshed because I had read, even memo-rized that verse years ago, but this time I felt as if this was the first time I had read it. I wanted to relish it and go through it slowly, tasting every sweet morsel.

God, the Source of all hope...

God, the *original* of all hope. God, the *rise* of all hope when His Son, Jesus, *arose* three days after He was killed on a cross. God, You are the source of *all* hope—not "most hope" or a "fraction of hope"—*all* hope. Any and all of the hope I've ever had in my life is from You, Lord, Who gives hope away freely and abundantly.

...will fill you completely with joy and peace...

Lord, You will not fill me just a little bit, partially, or almost all the way with joy and peace, but fully.

You will not fill me with sadness or melancholy, anxiety or war, fear or harm. Instead, you are the Prince of Peace and full of joy which You'll fill my soul with, too.

...because you trust Him.

God, I know, that I know, that I know that You are who You say You are.

Through Jesus, I know I can trust You.

Through Him, I know I am able.

Deep down, even though storms can shake me up, I choose to trust You. You are my Protector, and thank You for sheltering me under Your wing.

You will overflow with confident hope...

You will not fill me just halfway or right below the rim, Lord, but You will fill me with more confident hope than I can hold on my own. You are the One who gives me hope, not the world.

You do not fill me with a wary hope, with a little bit of hope, or false hope in worldly things. Instead, You give me more confident hope than I think I have and more than–I–know–what–to–do–with hope.

...by the power of the Holy Spirit.

Because of You, Lord, I do not need to search for power, buy power, or be powerful—but only by Your strength, I can do anything.

Please forgive me when I try to take control and have power over circumstances and other people. There is power in humility, and Your power is mighty to save!

In the Name of Jesus, Amen.

Prayer is life-saving. Prayer can calm the storms swirling inside of us and all around us. When God first created humans, He did for the pleasure to commune and to have a sweet relationship with us so that He can share His overflowing love. From the beginning of time, when God created humankind, we see in Genesis 2 that he had a relationship with Adam. They talked with each other and listened to everything from God instructing Adam not to eat the fruit from the one specific tree to letting Adam name all the different animals. After the fall, when Adam and Eve sinned against God for the first time, He did take the Garden of Eve away from them but did not take away communion with them. God desired to have a relationship with His people to keep intimate conversations and show care for each other. God has not changed. He is the same yesterday, today, and forever as stated in Hebrew 13:8.

So, prayer is pretty special to God, and He will make Himself known to us so we can have any conversation with Him whatsoever. We can cry out to him for protection, seek His wisdom, rejoice in His presence, even share our frustrations and broken hearts with Him. The intimacy deepens when we confess our sins and change our course to become closer to Him. Through prayer, God created languages for us to live life to its fullest with joy and peace. He wants our words of prayer to pour out as our souls pour out to Him. We can trust Him, for He is our Source of hope in this stormy world when we feel like we've been swept up and torn up by all the debris swirling around us.

May we put our hope and trust in God alone as He calms our storms.

Personal Reflections

What has been a storm in your life? It can be one you're in or one you've overcome. How are you, or did you weather through it emotionally?

What is one of your favorite verses in the Bible or your "life verse"? Read it and allow the Holy Spirit to expand on the meaning and truth in the words of that verse. Then, take it apart, a few words at a time, and reflect on what they mean. It might include researching the origin of a word and its definition in Hebrew or Greek. Go through it slowly and prayerfully. I suggest writing it down to go back later and pray it again. This practice of meditating on God's Word is good for your soul.

Additional Scripture: Matthew 8:23–27, Acts 27:13–26, Psalm 148

Personal Expressions

Acrylic Pouring Project—as we've been thinking about storms, which includes pouring rain, this can be a project to express what is pouring out of your heart and mind to the Lord. For example, it could represent the rain during the storm or the sun that came out after it was over. The instructions are located in the Appendix at the back of this book.

🔊 **Listen to *Keep on Hoping* by Riley Clemmons**

Closing Prayer

Oh God, You can calm the storms outside and in my life to a whisper and still the waves. I trust You and Your Word that says when the storms of life come, the wicked are whirled away, but the godly have a lasting foundation. Help me to remember what Jesus taught: "Anyone who listens to my teaching and follows it is wise, like a person who builds a house on solid rock. But anyone who hears my teaching and doesn't obey it is foolish, like a person who builds a house on sand. When the rains and floods come, and the winds beat against that house, it will collapse with a mighty crash." Thank You for Your Word to instruct me and teach me the way I should go; thank You for counseling me with Your loving eye on me through Your Word. I want to meditate on Your unfailing love as I worship You. Amen.

**† (Psalm 107:29, Proverbs 10:25,
Matthew 7:24-27, Psalm 48:9)**

CHAPTER 22

Go to a Counselor

Opening Prayer

God, I pray that You would set this reader free. God, in Your power, would You help us fight the enemy hell-bend on destroying us and help us remember that the power to choose a different way is ours in You? And then help us give that away to a world aching for a new way to think and live. In Jesus's name, Amen.

† **Jennie Allen** *Get Out of Your Head:
Stopping the Spiral of Toxic Thoughts*[1]

For we know that all creation has been groaning as in the pains of childbirth right up to the present time. And we believers also groan, even though we have the Holy Spirit within us as a foretaste of future glory, for we long for our bodies to be released from sin and suffering. We, too, wait with eager hope for the day when God will give us our full rights as his adopted children, including the new bodies he has promised us. We were given this hope when we were saved. (If we already have something, we don't need to hope for it. But if we look forward to something we don't yet have, we must wait patiently and confidently.) † **Romans 8:22-25**

---

1 Jennie Allen. *Get Out of Your Head: Stopping the Spiral of Toxic Thoughts* (WaterBrook: Penguin Random House: 2020) p. 223

Story

"Fine, God. If You're going to be silent and not heal me, then I guess I'll schedule an appointment with my doctor and a counselor, and maybe *they* can make me better."

I didn't hear a whisper or feel a nudge that said, "No, don't," so, begrudgingly, I picked up my phone and made the calls. Depression had worn me down.

Maybe you've experienced this. Perhaps you are at the end of your rope—too exhausted to keep resisting. Or perhaps this can give you a better understanding of your loved one or friend who's going through a dark season.

Depression is not just a 21st-century growing condition. Brain-sickness goes way back in history. Thousands of years back, in fact. It goes back to when the enemy first introduced sin to Adam and Eve and all their descendants, including us.

As I mentioned earlier in chapter three, God states in Genesis 3:18 how we will have to live among thorns and thickets because of the enemy determined to steal, kill, and destroy us.[2] The thorns can be anything that pierces us, causing pain and suffering in this life. One of the thorns that afflict us can be depression. There are written records that describe people struggling with depression early in the Bible. King David, who ruled Israel, is one, and as we read in the previous chapter, Elijah did too and is evident when we read how he cried out to God, "I have had enough, Lord. Take my life. I am no better than my ancestors."

Elijah said these words after running as fast and far away from Jezebel because she had announced that she wanted him murdered. He had killed 450 of her false god Baal's prophets, and she wanted revenge. (1 Kings 19:1–2)

---

2 John 10:10

Looking back earlier in his life, Elijah was kind of a loner. Almost all of God's children had conformed to the world's desires. Not Elijah. He allowed his obedience to God to isolate him. The only one Elijah had to talk with about his struggles was God.

Elijah set an example for us. God *is* who we need to go to for comfort and peace. Sometimes, though, God comforts and heals us through other people.

I learned that the hard way.

At the beginning of this chapter, you read the words that went through my head one, dreary and cold, February afternoon. For more than two years, I secretly battled depressing head-on, by myself, with no other soldiers behind me. Ever since I had brain surgery, I have experienced a few seasons of depression. But through personal prayer and some time, I was lifted out of that pit.

Relief never lasted long. It is not always easy to tell someone else what you're struggling with within your mind and heart. It can be embarrassing; we worry that it shows weakness and a lack of faith. Admitting we're struggling can make us fearful that people will look at us differently and treat us differently like we have leprosy. I think that's what Elijah experienced, too.

When it came to that February afternoon, when I expressed my built-up frustration with God, I felt abandoned and neglected by Him. He had not answered my prayer the way I wanted it answered. I didn't want to get on an anti-depressant medicine; I didn't want to ask my supervisor for time off work to go to a counseling session. I thought everyone in my circumference saw me as a joyful person. I didn't want them to see me as a woman of faith become a woman of faithlessness. But that is what I had become.

For several reasons, I had never been to a counselor. One, because I thought I had never needed one. Two, most of my adult life, telling other people my personal thoughts and feelings was a no-no according to my standards; I kept things to myself because it was my goal always to be a "good girl." Three, because I didn't want people to think I was "losing it." If they found out I was going to a psychiatrist, they might think I was unstable. Four, I didn't want to disappoint my family.

Surrendering those false narratives was not easy. Surrendering anything usually isn't easy. Grumbling, I slowly tapped the numbers on my phone to a Christian counselor that a trusted person recommended.

One week later, I walked into the basement of a building for my first counseling session. The dark waiting room had one small window covered with a darkening shade. Two lamps with dim bulbs gave enough light to find a place to sit. However, it did not feel like a warm welcome. I wanted to look around, but I stared at my phone because I didn't want anyone to see me.

Finally, after five minutes of waiting, which felt like 50, the counselor opened a door and called my name. Stepping out of that dim room, it was almost blinding as I walked into another room filled with light from the sun as its rays shined through large windows that covered most of the wall.

Still reluctant, I followed the counselor into his office. There were two large sofas to choose to sit on, two windows, a desk, a dresser, a large, bouncy exercise ball, a bookshelf full of books by authors I also read, and many framed pictures and documents on the walls. It felt homier.

After gazing around the room, my eyes landed on the counselor. He was sitting on the exercise ball with a clipboard in his hand, and surprisingly, a Cheshire-cat grin covered half of his face.

I couldn't help but smile back.

The tension in my shoulders and neck somewhat relaxed, and my healing journey began. There were no smiles on my face at every appointment. More often than not, there were tears and blank stares as I wrestled with my thoughts and feelings.

I sometimes wonder if Elijah's life would've been different if he'd made an effort to talk to someone about his loneliness and depression. Of course, ultimately, we have the Lord to speak to through prayer and be comforted and lifted by His Spirit dwelling in us, but God also gives other people the gift of good listening skills and sound counsel, whom He wants to work through.

Before going to a counselor, I had not interacted well with my pain. I suppressed and concealed my sadness and my self-rejecting thoughts. My heart, mind, and soul had become a tangled-up mess, like a ball of twisted rubber bands. I'd been resistant to meeting with a counselor for most of my adult years. I only wish I had not been so stubborn and had called for help years sooner.

We can spend countless hours trying to untangle our messy feelings and emotions, but more than often, we make things more tangled, and we need someone to help us get untangled. Jesus is the only One who can untangle all those rubber bands, and He authorizes people with the gifts of counseling and training to do the work. While guided in the healing process, I became aware that the dull, brown rubber bands in that ball were actually bright, colorful ones when dusted off.

Then the bands begin to untangle as we start interacting with our pain. Jesus did. He understands how you feel because he experienced depression, too. When Jesus saw people suffering and grieving, he cried with those who cried. Often, he abandoned his disciples early in the morning to be alone; and while in prayer, Jesus more than likely cried out loud to his Abba for Jerusalem, His Kingdom, because they were broken and hurting.

Jesus didn't hide or ignore his sad feelings. He didn't worry about what other people thought of him. Nor did he disguise his pain and sorrow like we tend to do. Instead, he cried when he needed to because he knew that was the healthy thing to do.

Jesus gave us the example that it is OK to have all the emotions we do have, and then how we're to work through them.

As David wrote this Psalm, he also knew the necessity of having counsel sometimes in our lives:

> *"I will instruct you and teach you in the way you should go; I will counsel you with my loving eye on you."* † **(Psalm 32:8 NIV)**

Whether the Wonderful Counselor counsels you through His Spirit, through His Word, through a licensed counselor, a pastor, or a friend, know that you matter—to Him and the people in your life. Seek counsel and healing. Untangle those rubber bands. It's worth it. You're worth it.

Personal Reflections

I once saw this statement: *"If you rearrange the letters in 'depression', you'll get 'I Pressed On.' Your current situation is not your final destination."* So what are some simple, tangible ways you can press on today?

If you're struggling with a biological predisposition towards depression or physiological imbalance (a mental unwellness), are you willing to talk to someone about your sadness or anxiety? A friend, a pastor, or a counselor? If yes, keep doing that. If no, pray and ask God to give you the boldness to seek help.

Additional Scripture: Hebrews 5:7–8, Psalm 143, 1 Kings 19: 1–13

Personal Expressions

Enjoy a rubber band project. Instructions are in the appendix. While you're engaged in this project, think about all the rubber bands wrapped around the paper resisting the color to show on the paper and how our lives can be a tangled mess. Pay attention to your feelings when you're adding color. How does it make you feel? After the paint dries, remove the rubber bands one by one, untangling them from your art, and think about how God, our Wonderful Counselor, helps us untangle our messy emotions, sometimes with the help of a counselor or a listening loved one. Once they're all off, look at your artwork, unique, colorful, and freeing. What used to be dull paper is now vibrant and life-giving.

🔊 **Listen to** *Never Lost* **by CeCe Winans**

Closing Prayer

Lord, I call to You, but You do not seem to answer. Every night I lift my voice, but I find no relief. How long must I struggle with anguish in my soul, with sorrow in my heart every day? Yet I know You are my Helper, and You are with me forever. Please guide me with Your counsel to the right source for help. Help me get out of bed each morning, to live each day with hope as I remember You understand how I feel. Please protect me and enable me to stand today. You, Lord, promise in Your Word that You are close to the brokenhearted and save those who are crushed in spirit. Please don't break that promise with me. Amen.

**This chapter may have stirred up emotions you're struggling to express. I encourage you to seek a counselor. There are often ones through your job/work benefits, and there are several online counseling services these days. I recommend a Christian counselor if you can have access to one.

CHAPTER 23

Tell a Friend

Opening Prayer

LORD, high and holy, meek and lowly,
Thou has brought me to the valley of vision,
where I live in the depths but see thee in the heights;
hemmed in by mountains of sin I behold thy glory.
Let me learn by paradox
That the way down is the way up,
That to be low is to be high,
That the broken heart is the healed heart,
That the contrite spirit is the rejoicing spirit,
That the repenting souls the victorious soul,
That to have nothing is to possess all,
That to bear the cross is to wear the crown,
That to give is to receive, that the valley is the place of vision.
Lord, in the daytime stars can be seen from deepest wells,
And the deeper the wells, the brighter thy stars shine;
Let me find thy light in my darkness,
Thy life in my death, 'thy joy in my sorrow,
Thy grace in my sin,
Thy riches in my poverty
Thy glory in my valley. † **The Valley of Vision**[1]

---

1 *The Valley of Vision: A Collection of Puritan Prayers & Devotions* edited by Arthur Bennett (The Banner of Truth Trust, 1975), xxiv

O Lord, hear me as I pray;
pay attention to my groaning.
 Listen to my cry for help, my King and my God,
for I pray to no one but you.
 Listen to my voice in the morning, Lord.
Each morning I bring my requests to you and wait expectantly.

† Psalm 5:1–3

Story

She could probably hear the thump of my heart beating across the room. I didn't want others to know I was deep in this dark valley of the soul. In my mind, burdening a friend who already has significant obstacles in her own life with my problems is not being a good friend. That winter afternoon, I turned my head from looking out at the leafless trees inhaled, hoping to get a deep breath before I spoke. But my chest pounded more, robbing me of my intention. She was still waiting, and she knew how to read me. Between my anxious body language and the unusually negative comments that frequently came out of my mouth lately, she knew something was going on with me. Oh, how I don't like being vulnerable, but I knew I needed to do this.

Reluctantly, I quietly began to speak, "Sarah, you may...." And suddenly, the bottom of my eyes pooled with tears. "You may have already noticed, but I'm struggling from depression." Unexpectantly, I was then able to inhale deeply. After the words came out, I looked up to see her reaction. Her eyes of compassion encouraged me to keep talking. I continued, "For almost two years now. I just told my husband last week. I know I probably shouldn't have kept it in this long without confiding about it with someone, but I didn't want to burden anyone. Plus, I was hoping God would answer my prayer for healing, but I'm at the point now where I've given up and don't think He's going to answer my prayer, at least the way I want it answered."

Saying those few sentences brought a wave of relief. I hadn't realized how much bottled-up tension I'd been holding in my chest. Why is it so difficult for me to express my feelings? I have many dear friends and family who I know would pray for me if I asked them to, but shame silenced my voice every time I even thought about sharing my struggle. Now, I wished I hadn't waited so long.

Sarah continued to listen, ask questions, and share some of her struggles, too. Then, before she needed to go, she prayed for me— and one of her gifts is prayer. Tears returned as gratitude-filled some of my hollow soul. She's a dear friend who knew what I needed. Lately, my prayers had felt repetitive and shallow— Sarah's prayer was authentic. The words were what I needed to hear; I had been trying to pray, I had been wrestling to believe, and through Sarah's prayer, I offered them to God.

The following morning was like any other morning. Dragging myself out of bed took a lot of energy, but somehow, I showered, made my kids breakfast, packed their lunches, and made it out the door in time to get to work.

Ding.

I glanced at my phone in the car console to see a text from Sarah. At the stoplight, I read, "I'm on my way to work, but I heard this song when I was getting ready this morning, and it made me think of you. I hope it encourages you, and know that I'll be praying for you." Attached to her message was a link to a song video. I don't remember what the song was, but I won't forget the tears that rolled down my cheeks as I drove to work that morning listening to that song. *Thank you, Jesus.* That's about the only thing I could pray.

The next morning on my way to work, Sarah texted again with different uplifting words and another song. And again, the third day, with another note and song. She did this for *a year.* Monday through Friday, every morning around 7:45 am, my friend gave me hope. Monday through Thursday were Christian songs, but Fridays were always a surprise, usually a fun 80's song from our childhood days that made me tap my feet, sing, and smile, all of which had become rare expressions for me. Sarah gave me the gift of worship because she knew I struggled with it on my own. She made it accessible for me because she knew I needed help.

What amazed me the most in all of this was that she was also experiencing life in a valley. Yet, because of our friendship and her love for God, Sarah persistently checked on me, staying by my side. I'll never be able to thank her enough for being a companion in the valley with me and for bringing along some music and conversations to remind me that I wasn't alone.

In the books of 1 and 2 Kings, we can read about a friendship between Elijah and Elisha. God told him to appoint Elisha as His next prophet during Elijah's ministry. It would be a while before it was time for Elisha to take on that responsibility, though, giving time for Elijah to train Elisha about being a prophet of the Lord. Throughout their time together, their mentorship developed into a friendship. Elisha and Elijah experienced life together. They share the highs and lows, the joys and disappointments, the confidence and fear, the holy and the worldly—together.

When the time came for Elijah to leave the earth, God's Spirit instructed him to go to the town of Bethel. Elijah told Elisha his plan to go to Bethel and not go with him, but Elisha refused and went with him—as a friend. Elisha told Elijah, "'As surely as the Lord lives and you yourself live, I will never leave you!' So, they went down together to Bethel." (2 Kings 2:2)

God brought them together for many reasons, but I think one of them is the importance of friendship. Elijah struggled with depression, anxiety, and loneliness, so God put Elisha in his life to encourage and be there for him. Elisha would not leave his side, and Elijah didn't dispute or insist that he go alone—he accepted Elisha's companionship. That makes me think how in my life, I've had friends offer to be by my side when I'm about to embark on a journey or when I'm in the thick of something difficult. I often say, "No, I'm fine. I can do this on my own," but secretly, I'm hoping she'll refuse my answer. Then, when she says, "No, I'm not taking 'no' for an answer," my heart breathes a sigh of relief because I really do want her by my side. I just have a hard time asking for it.

The display of Elijah and Elisha's sincere friendship doesn't end there, though. We just saw how Elisha professed his friendship to Elijah, but Elijah turns around and wants to offer his to Elisha as well. Elijah seemed to know that the Lord was going to take him into heaven soon because he asked Elisha in 2 Kings 2:9, "Tell me what I can do for you before I am taken away."

That right there, friend, is what we call friendship with compassion. If I had woken up one morning with a strong hunch that today was the day God would take me to heaven, my emotions would be heightened and multiplied. Anticipating worries of the unknowns, wanting to be with the ones I love, stressed because there are things I wish I had done—or not done—and the list can go on. Would I have thought that morning, "What can I do *for* my family and friends today before I leave?"

Well, Elijah did think about serving his friend because God's Spirit lived inside of him, even though he had been struggling deep in the valley. He was not thinking only of himself. Before Elijah was taken away, he asked Elisha what he could do for him. That question echoed 850 years later from Jesus when he asked many sick, disabled, or "living in the deep valley" that same question. *"Tell me what I can do for you before I am taken away?"* (Mark 10:51)

Author Brennan Manning wrote,

"The etymology of the word *compassion* lies in two Latin words, *cum,* and *patior,* meaning 'to suffer with, to endure with, to struggle with, and to partake of the hunger, nakedness, loneliness, pain, and broken dreams of our brothers and sisters in the human family. Commitment to Jesus Christ without compassion for his people is a lie."

Manning goes on to say, "Every time the Gospel mentions that Jesus was moved with the deepest emotions or felt sorry for people, it led to his doing something—physical or inner healing, deliverance or exorcism, feeding the hungry crowds or intercessory prayer."[2]

Elijah didn't give up even though he suffered from loneliness, people pursuing to kill him, and wanting his own life to end. He didn't think only of himself even if he didn't always feel joy-full. That is a testament to Elijah asking the Holy Spirit to live in him because it is in our weakness that God works through us as He carries us through each day. Because of God's Spirit inside of him, even if he did not always feel His presence, he persevered, living and working in the valley. He knew that God was for him and with him, and he loved God, showing that by his obedience.

God gave Elijah a friend and companion to be by his side in the valley, who was willing to do the hard work for the Kingdom. God, who became incarnate, and walked this earth, gave each of us a friend who is compassionate about us and wants to be our companion in the valley. His name is Jesus. He is the One who knows what it's like more than any of us to suffer. Therefore, He doesn't want us to experience that alone. Often when we're in the valley, we're given the gift of vision to see Jesus in unexpected and surprising ways, including, and especially, through friendships.

---

2 Brennan Manning. *A Glimpse of Jesus: The Stranger to Self-Hatred*, (New York: HarperOne, 2003) p. 124–126

Personal Reflections

Is it easy or difficult for you to share your mental health (whether good or bad) with a friend? Why is that? Do you wish you had done the opposite? Why?

Write about a time in your life when you were in the valley. How did you live in the valley? If you're still in the valley, what are some ways God has shown his compassion for you while in this season?

Additional Scripture: 1 Kings 19: 1–21, 2 Kings 2:1–18, Luke 3:1–6

Personal Expressions

What is your perspective of being in a valley? Listen to the song *Valleys Fill First* by Caedmon's Call and pay attention to the lyrics. Which line or lines grabbed your attention the most? Why? Take out your journal and create a picture or image which reflects those words of what a valley experience is like for you. Maybe include the words in the project.

Closing Prayer

O Lord, hear me as I pray; listen to my cry for help, my King and my God, for I pray to no one but You. Listen to my voice in the morning, Lord. Each morning I bring my requests to You and wait expectantly. Thousands upon thousands are waiting in the valley, but Lord, You will be a refuge for Your people. Even when I walk through the darkest valley, I will not be afraid, for You are close beside me. Your rod and Your staff protect and comfort me. You are the Lily of the Valley, and I will trust You here in this valley. Amen.

† **(Psalm 5:1–3, Joel 3:14,16, Psalm 23:4, Song of Solomon 2:1)**

CHAPTER 24

Share Your Struggle

Opening Prayer

Dear Lord, forgive me in that so much of my religion is concerned with myself. I want harmony with thee. I want peace of mind. I want health of body—and so I pray.

Forgive me, for I have made thee the means and myself the end.

I know it will take long to wean me from this terrible self-concern, but O God, help me, for hell can be nothing else but a life on which self is the centre. † **Leslie Weatherhead**[1]

All praise to God, the Father of our Lord Jesus Christ. God is our merciful Father and the source of all comfort. He comforts us in all our troubles so that we can comfort others. When they are troubled, we will be able to give them the same comfort God has given us. For the more we suffer for Christ, the more God will shower us with his comfort through Christ.

† **2 Corinthians 1:3–5**

Story

When I pushed "play," the video started, and I sat down to watch it with a group of women while enjoying some movie theater

---

1 *The HarperCollins Book of Prayers*, comp. by Robert Van de Weyer. (NewYork: HarperCollins Publishers, 1993) p. 382

popcorn. Fifty minutes later, before the actual end of the video, the screen cut out, leaving me to conclude what the speaker on the video was going to say. I watched the video before showing it to the women at our church, so thankfully, I had some idea of closing the message.

Being one of the leaders for this group, I helped plan monthly events. We'd work through various series, and the theme we were using was *Tell Your HIStory.* A few women shared their story of faith, which usually centered around a struggle or suffering, and how God had redeemed them through it. I had no plan to share mine. My role was to push play for a video to watch. Since July was a month with lower attendance, we decided to show a pre-recorded teaching by some influential female Christian authors and speakers instead of having someone at our church share her story.

In the small parlor room, dimly lit, with a few rows of women looking at me, I managed to close for the speaker, but as I was speaking, I felt a nudge from God that I wasn't expecting and certainly wasn't wanting to do. God asked me to tell the women my story about how I'd struggled with depression the past couple of years. I cringed at the idea.

"Nooo...Lord, it's embarrassing, shameful, something I've tried to hide—I don't want to confess that here. I don't want to show–and–tell about my ugly infection." But before I could complain any longer, I described for them my battle with depression over the past two and a half years. Looking back, I don't recall much of what I said. Still, when it was over, I *do* remember taking a deep breath, inhaling the grace of God who got me through it, silently thanking Him for the opportunity, and feeling an incredible sense of peace and joy that I was not expecting. It was freeing to share my story.

As women were collecting their belongings to leave, one woman came up to me and told me this was the first time she'd been to one of our church's women's events and thanked me for my transparency. Then, she reached out and hugged me, looked me in the eyes, and said, she sees the light of Jesus in me.

When she turned around to leave, another woman was waiting to talk with me. I greeted her and thanked her for coming. She then told me how she has struggled with depression for 20 years. She's kept that secret inside and hadn't felt comfortable telling anyone. But hearing me tell my story of suffering encouraged her. She wasn't the only one.

It is important to tell someone else when you're struggling. If you're like me, that can be a struggle. Yet, God also showed me that not sharing my story could become a pride issue if I'm not careful in His loving grace. I thought of several times when I had the opportunity to share my faith and "show my scar" with someone but didn't. I gave myself excuses because I worried what they'd think of me: a goody-two-shoes, holier-than-thou, or even hypocrite. Or I've used this one: I don't know what to say, and whatever I say won't come outright. I also feared I wouldn't be accepted or even looked down upon if they knew I felt unwell on the inside. Even though I was struggling, I surely didn't want to appear that way because, self-consciously, I just wanted every-one to like me. And who would like me if they knew I suffered from depression? I had more desire for humans' approval than I did about sharing the grace and healing power of Jesus.

As we've read in this book and the Bible, we can see the Bible is full of stories of people who internally struggled through all kinds of difficult things in their lives.

Abraham had to wait 85 years of his life until God gave him the son He had promised him.

Sarai had been childless her whole life and had given up hope in ever becoming pregnant. When she finally did, she laughed in her husband's face and at God because she could hardly believe it.

God's people lived enslaved in Egypt for generations.

Gideon had been living in oppression for many years and needed constant assurance that God would help him overcome his insecurity.

Elijah was one of the most profound prophets during his time, whom God worked through even as he struggled with depression.

Job lost all his belongings, his family died, and he became ill with a disease.

David committed adultery, causing guilt that almost took him out.

Jeremiah was ignored, scoffed at, and rejected, which devastated him and led him to anger towards God to almost give up his ministry.

God's people somehow survived for roughly 400 years with little spiritual guidance, no word from the prophets, and God's seeming silence. And those are just a few examples from the Old Testament. But unfortunately, the struggles did not end there.

If they had never told someone their story or showed their scars—we wouldn't know how God saved them and loved them and how they continued to persevere, even though it was hard.

Your story matters.

Sharing the story of your scars may make you feel ugly or ashamed, but in truth, it makes you more beautiful. Shattering experiences can turn out to be a beautiful display of grace and healing for yourself and others. That summer night, I remember telling the women how I was grateful for the foundation I had growing up in church and my relationship with God for several years. I said how grateful I am to know God's Word even though I didn't feel His presence in that season of my life. Even though my stomach felt like a knot was in it, afterward, I experienced joy having given God the glory.

When we share our stories of how Jesus met us in our pain and remains with us as it scars, we are giving our testimony. K.J. Ramsey writes:

> *"Such testimony is what we desperately need because, without it, we do not see Jesus clearly, either for ourselves or for others. Hearing that testimony clears our ears to hear the gospel even through the pain and not only apart from it. Hearing it, we gain courage in our faith to face our particular trials and tribulations, our fears and frustrations."*[2]

I encourage you to share your story and show your scar. It's not easy, but it's healing.

One afternoon, at a counseling session, my counselor told me about a form of Japanese art called *kintsugi*, which means "golden repair." An artist takes broken pottery and repairs it by gluing it back together, then brushing gold lacquer onto the edges of the fractured pieces, highlighting the cracks. This process takes time. Between the application of each layer of lacquer, the edges must be sanded over and over. Doesn't that sound familiar? Doesn't it sometimes feel like our daily struggles are rubbing us raw? Struggling in similar situations like people in the Bible did, or the shame of needing approval, or battle scars from broken relationships, just to name a few. How much longer does it have to last? With patience and precision, God is the Artist who will work to create our lives into the piece of art He has in mind for us. He has an extraordinary gift for creating something beautiful out of brokenness.

Even if you feel scared, embarrassed, ashamed, or timid, still reveal your scar. Tell your story of how God is the hero. Show and tell someone about the art of your precious scars. Sharing your story to someone who needs to hear it is like giving them a gift of art created by the Master Artist Himself. As Paul described in

---

2   K.J. Ramsey. *This Too Shall Last: Finding Grace When Suffering Lingers,* (Michigan: Zondervan Reflective, 2020) p. 17

2 Corinthians 1:4–5, *"When they are troubled, we will be able to give them the same comfort God has given us. For the more we suffer for Christ, the more God will shower us with His comfort through Christ."*

Personal Reflections

Pray, asking God to give you the strength and courage to tell someone your story. Ask Him to show you who that person should be. Then, tell that person over coffee, during bible study, during a work break, or in a phone conversation about your struggle. Or maybe God has nudged you to go to a licensed counselor if needed. There is healing power for yourself when telling someone else.

Reach out to someone you think is going through a similar struggle as you have. Share how God has been recreating your heart and soul and encourage her to trust that she is not alone.

Additional Scripture: Hebrews 2:1–3, Matthew 5:1–12, John 20:24–29

Personal Expressions

Doodle a picture of a piece of broken pottery with markers or crayons and go over the broken crack with a type of gold color. Underneath write one of the Scripture verses listed above or remind you why your story matters. Or, if you're up for the challenge, research the process of how to create kintsugi pieces of art and make one for yourself!

🔊 **Listen to *Scars* by TobyMac**

Closing Prayer

God, the generous Grace-giver, who opposes the proud but gives grace to the humble, I give You praise. I have thanks to You, for You are good, Your faithful love endures forever. You ask me in Your Word, "Has the Lord redeemed you? Then speak out! Tell others he has redeemed you". Yes, You have redeemed me, Lord, and I am not ashamed of this Good News about Your Son, Jesus Christ. It is Your power at work, saving everyone who believes in You. I am not ashamed to bear on my body the scars that show I belong to You, Your Son, and Your Spirit—Your Trinity who lives in me. Lord, may everyone share the story of Your wonderful goodness and sing with joy about Your righteousness. Amen

**† (James 4:6, Psalm 107:2, Romans 1:16,
Galatians 6:17, Psalm 145:7)**

PART FIVE

Becoming a
Masterpiece

CHAPTER 25

He Waits

Opening Prayer

Lord, slip up on us today. Get past our defenses, our worries, our concerns. Gently open our souls and speak your Word into them. We believe you want to do it, and we wait for you to do it now. In your Name, Amen.

† Dallas Willard *Life Without Lack*[1]

Dear brothers and sisters, be patient as you wait for the Lord's return. Consider the farmers who patiently wait for the rains in the fall and in the spring. They eagerly look for the valuable harvest to ripen. You, too, must be patient. Take courage, for the coming of the Lord is near.

† James 5:7-8

Story

"Don't go away until I come back.[2] Wait right there."

In the chapter *Doubting God*, we read how farmer Gideon encountered an angelic Visitor while threshing wheat. In Judges chapter six, the Visitor, or God, told Gideon to go in the strength he had and save Israel from the Midianites. Doubting his ability, calling,

---

1 Dallas Willard. *Life Without Lack: Living in the Fullness of Psalm 23*, (Nashville: Nelson Books, 2018), xiii
2 Judges 6:18

and ultimately, the Lord, Gideon asked the Visitor to show him a sign to prove that He is the Lord and wait right where He was until he came back. Gideon needed to know if the Lord was serious, and this wasn't a dream or a joke.

So, the Lord waited while Gideon went home and cooked a goat and baked a loaf of bread from scratch. When it was finally ready, Gideon hurried back to the Lord, placed the meal in front of him, and instead of picking the food up with His hands, the Lord held His staff and had the tip of it touch the meat and bread, immediately causing it to go up in flames. It was right then when Gideon believed he was in the presence of the Lord.

The fact that the food caught on fire didn't catch my attention as much as Gideon asking God to wait.

How often do you ask God to wait?—I asked myself that question. If you're like me, my first thought is usually the other way around. *I'm* usually asking, "How long do I have to wait, Lord?"

That four-letter word can feel like a curse. Wait. How many hours of our lives have we been waiting? As toddlers, we must wait our turn, then wait to get old enough to graduate from sitting in the back seat to the car's front seat, then wait to get a driver's license. We wait in bumper-to-bumper traffic, at the grocery store check-out line, to get a call from the doctor, to get asked on a date, to get married, to be a parent, to get a job you love or a promotion you've wanted.

As believers, waiting for mourning to end, for an answered prayer, for a wounded heart to heal, for trust to strengthen, for our souls reignited, and joy to flourish is not any easier. I once heard someone say not to ask God for patience because He'll answer that prayer with a time of waiting, so you'll have the opportunity to practice patience.

Waiting isn't something people like to do. However, if we're not careful, we can become agitated or grumpy when waiting. I admit, when things aren't going the way I want, mainly if it includes waiting while suffering or struggling, I want it to end—right now. Even though I may appear to be patient on the outside, internally, I'm allowing impatience to fester. Frustration tries to gain control of my mind, allowing resentment to take root. A dire, unanswered prayer can also make us feel rejected, hurt, discouraged, or forgotten, whether two days, two weeks, two years or two decades.

Have you ever thought about how God might feel when it comes to waiting? He waited while Gideon took a couple of hours to cook Him a meal or offer Him a sacrifice. He waited until Gideon finally agreed to battle the Midianites. God waited for thousands of years, watching His people fall short of the Law and sending His Son. He still waits today to return to earth a second time once the Gospel is proclaimed in all corners and nations of the world. (Matthew 24:14) *God cares enough to wait.*

He waits until we open our eyes each morning because He's thrilled to spend the day with us. He'll never stop waiting until we sit still for a short period of our time each day so He can relish some one-on-one time with us. He waits until we stop talking and begin listening to what He has to say. He waits until His perfect timing to teach us something specific that He wants us to learn. God waits until we realize that what we've got is not ours but His, and we faithfully give a portion of it back to Him. He waits for us to break a habit, make a change, and ultimately trust Him. Have you noticed God doesn't wait until we've pulled our lives together, though? Before understanding God's abundant grace, we often think He must wait while we try to fix our problems, sins, and selves before we can put even our pinky toe on the King's carpet that leads to His throne. But that is not true. His mercy and the sacrifice of His Son, Jesus, who died for you and me, is the reason why we don't have to wait any longer to experience His compassion and love for us.

And that's just a teeny-tiny fraction of the total amount of time God has waited. If there's anyone who knows what it's like to wait, it's God, Himself. Ever since Adam and Eve sinned and ate the forbidden fruit, God has waited. He's been patiently waiting for our sakes. He believes it's worth waiting until every nation or people group has heard the Good News of His Kingdom.[3] God's patiently waiting because He is love.[4]

Peter described God's patience when he wrote,

> *"The Lord isn't really being slow about his promise, as some people think. No, he is being patient for your sake. He does not want anyone to be destroyed but wants everyone to repent."*

So, we have the opportunity to become more like Jesus when we wait with patience. Every person has countless times to practice this unfavorable instruction. When I'm impatiently waiting in line at the store, sometimes I'm reminded of Jesus' disciples and wonder what it would have been like for them on the Passover, the Sabbath, the Saturday after Jesus's crucifixion. This man—who performed miracles, told stories about the Kingdom, who displayed love and compassion for people, especially the marginalized, whom Peter called "The Messiah—the Son of the Living God"[5]—was killed, so what in the world were they supposed to do? I cannot imagine how long that Saturday must have felt. Have you ever thought about how we are daily living a long Saturday until Jesus comes again or when we go to be with Him in heaven? While we're reluctantly waiting for a prayer to be answered, God, Himself is working and waiting for people to accept His gift of redemption and Jesus' sacrifice as their salvation so that as many people as possible will be with Him in His Kingdom when He returns.

As believers, we must trust God's timing and believe that waiting is a process to make us depend upon Him and trust Him whole-heartedly. We need to believe that God trusts us, His disciples.

---

3   Matthew 24:14
4   1 John 4:8
5   Matthew 16:16

Like Gideon's experience with his Visitor, God continues to wait until we realize how much He trusts us and can use us to go into the battles of this world. He also knows it will take some time. But, when we're in a season in life where hope is hard to find, and we don't see ourselves as capable of doing work for the Lord, He promises us He's with us and will never leave us. God wants us to know that truth because He trusts us with it and wants us to trust Him.

The Visitor said, *"I will stay here and wait until you return. I'm not going anywhere."*

That's what God said to Gideon, *and that's what He says to you and me,* and all who are yet to invite Jesus to live in their hearts.

"I'll *wait. For you. I promise."*

Personal Reflections

What are you waiting for today? It can be something tangible, an answer to a specific prayer, or both. Remember, when we wait for something, sometimes we wait with impatience, and sometimes we wait with anticipation, like a vacation, having lunch with a friend, or Christmas day! List all you're waiting for, followed by how waiting for it makes you feel.

Often you don't realize, but beauty and goodness can be found in the process of waiting. It can increase your faith, draw you closer to God, and make you a more resilient person. Think of a time or two, currently or in the past, when waiting helped you become more like Christ.

Additional Scripture: Luke 12:35–40, Philippians 3:17–21, Psalm 37:1–10

Personal Expressions

If possible, go online and search for the image "On The Shore of Galilee" by C. Michael Dudash. This oil painting is of Jesus sitting and waiting based on John 21:1-14. Take some time and admire the art. Pay attention to the colors and textures. What is your favorite part of the painting and why? What do you think Jesus is thinking in this picture? Does he appear to be waiting patiently or impatiently for the fish to finish cooking or for the disciples to notice he's on the shore? Take a little bit of time to enjoy the painting while you thank God for waiting for you.

🔊 **Listen to *Waiting Here for You* by Christy Nockels**

Closing Prayer

Lord, I am worn out waiting for Your rescue, but I have put my hope in Your Word. My eyes are straining to see Your promises come true, yet I know You are my strength, and in Your unfailing love, You will stand with me. Even creation has been groaning as in the pains of childbirth right up to the present time along with Your believers who wait in eager hope for the day when You will give us our full rights as Your adopted children. Lord, You do not want me to forget this one thing: A day is like a thousand years to You, and a thousand years is like a day. You aren't really being slow about Your promise. No, You are being patient for our sake. You don't want anyone to be destroyed but want everyone to repent. While I wait for Your return, help me to make every effort to be found living a peaceful life that is pure and blameless in Your sight. While I wait to hear the answer to my requests, I desire to be joyful always, continue to pray, and be thankful in all circumstances because that is Your will for those who belong to Christ Jesus. Amen.

† **(Psalm 119:81-82, Psalm 69:9-10, Romans 8:20-23, 2 Peter 3:8-9, 14, 1 Thessalonians 5:16-18)**

CHAPTER 26

He Cares

Opening Prayer

God who rests,

It is difficult for us to imagine a Christ who, having all power and capacity to heal others, still at times walked away. Who napped unapologetically in the face of danger. Give us the courage to rest. The holy audacity to do absolutely nothing at all. And as we do, allow us to hold vigil for the tombs of this world while honoring that we are neither savior nor slave. Grant us a slowness that allows us to feel what hurts and makes healing possible. Let our rest be our liberation.

† Cole Authur Riley[1]

"Then Jesus said, 'Come to me, all of you who are weary and carry heavy burdens, and I will give you rest. Take my yoke upon you. Let me teach you, because I am humble and gentle at heart, and you will find rest for your souls. For my yoke is easy to bear, and the burden I give you is light.'" **† Matthew 11:28-30**

Story

My face looked like a Star Trek Klingon. Literally. Raised ripples of skin covered my forehead. It wasn't Halloween or a costume

---

1 Cole Arthur Riley. "Black Liturgies," 2021, https://colearthurriley.com/writing/project-one-64g3t

party. I had no idea what was happening to my face, but I did know it felt like piercing, hot needles trying to escape from the inside of my head. I assumed the cause was an allergic reaction to medicine a new doctor prescribed me when I went to his office with a constant headache for three days. The doctor said it was a sinus infection.

Two days later, my headache worsened, and painful blisters had formed on my forehead.

A friend of ours, who happens to be an orthopedic physician's assistant, stopped by that night because he wanted to check on our 5-year-old daughter who had broken her ankle just six days earlier—the same day my headache started. His eyes opened wide when he saw my face.

"Umm, Beth, you need to go to the emergency room," he said calmly, yet seriously.

"What's happening to me?" I asked with a higher-pitched voice of concern.

"It looks like you have a bad case of shingles, and it's now getting into your eye."

After several miserable hours in the emergency room, the doctor said the same thing our friend said. "You've got a pretty serious case of shingles." My husband asked what could have triggered the dormant virus to activate. The doctor replied, "It's usually because of a low immune system. Have you been stressed lately? Stress causes your immune system to weaken."

Yes, the past several months were extremely stressful.

Eight months earlier, my mother-in-law underwent a stem-cell transplant because of cancer. A couple in our life was going through a difficult divorce, and we invited the mom and son to live with us for a little bit. Our 8-year-old son had taken a trip to the emergency room, too, when his friend clocked his forehead with a croquet mallet (by accident), resulting in several stitches. One of our church's pastors who taught a weekly Bible study for a few years had just announced she was moving out of town, and my heart was saddened because her teaching had encouraged me in my faith, and I didn't want that to end. My husband was in a season of challenges at work which added stress to our relationship, plus he was naturally concerned for his mom's health. The last straw was when our daughter broke her ankle. Considering all the stressful things happening at once, it's no surprise I was now suffering from shingles.

Unable to do anything else, I slept most of the following week. When I finally had gained enough energy, one afternoon, enjoying the warmth of the spring sun, I slowly walked down the driveway to the mailbox. Walking back to the house, I saw an envelope with familiar handwriting. A small smile formed on my deformed-looking face as I began reading the card from the woman who taught the Bible study. She had filled the blank card with her words of encouragement. One sentence particularly moved me: *"May you find yourself unexpectedly replenished and renewed during this 'enforced time of recovery."*

Enforced it was. Shingles was a painful blessing in disguise. It interrupted my life, forcing me to rest. Sometimes, God uses illness as an opportunity. Sometimes recovery is the only way to get us to rest. God knew I needed to rest and allowed a physical illness to make it happen.

Before my shingles outbreak, I had not been trusting the Lord— worrying, stressed, overcommitting myself with to-do's, prayer time was minimal, and I was not surrendering much in my life to Him. However, my experience with shingles taught me that stress, making lousy choices, and refusing rest causes anxiety, which—for me anyway—triggered shingles.

In our busy-is-good culture, rest is almost considered a curse. Taking time to rest is for the weak.

Studies have proven otherwise, though. Research shows that lack of physical and mental rest causes stress and exhaustion, weakens our immune system, changes our moods, and become less productive. On the other hand, studies also show how rest sparks our creativity, restores our mental energy, and improves short-term memory. God created us with the need for physical and mental downtime, and when we choose to stay busy and stressed, we suffer. It's almost as if God allows certain circumstances to put us in time-out. In time-out, or enforced rest, we're put in the position not only to heal, but it also puts us in the position to encounter resting in the Lord, which is the rest we often overlook and devalue.

Rest is so important to God; He set an example for us when He rested after the sixth day of Creation. When God finished creating planets, atoms, elephants, weather, and the first human, He rested.

By the seventh day, God had finished the work he had been doing, so he rested from all his work on the seventh day. Then God blessed the seventh day and made it holy because he rested from all the work of creating that he had done. (Genesis 2:2–4) NIV

It's worth noting that God did not *need* rest; He *chose* to rest. Our all-powerful, all-knowing, everywhere present God wasn't worn out or stressed. His rest on the seventh day is the first display of His compassion and care for us. Just like He worked six days and rested on the seventh, He wants us to practice that same liturgical rhythm because He knows we need it. We are humans made of flesh. He didn't create us like robots, just needing to be plugged into a socket to regain energy. Our bodies and minds are rejuvenated by resting physically, mentally, and spiritually. God is a God of rhythm. He created us to need food and sleep each day, designed four seasons and a calendar that includes months, weeks, and days—and one of those days He designated to rest.

When God gave Moses the Ten Commandments, rest is right on up there with the importance to not murder, steal, or have an affair.

"Remember the Sabbath day by keeping it holy. Six days you shall labor and do all your work, but the seventh day is a Sabbath to the Lord your God." (Exodus 20:8–10 NIV)

While extra physical rest is needed, that's not the only rest God wants us to practice every seventh day. Mental and spiritual rest are also necessary to have complete rest. The ritual of intentionally not worrying about the things on your mind or thinking of the upcoming week's to-do list allows our minds to rest. And not only that, but God also declares that Sabbath is a holy day. "God blessed the seventh day and made it holy." (Genesis 2:3) He blesses us when we make time for worship. God has given us the gift of the Sabbath because He loves us dearly and wants us to experience delight at least *one day each week*! What a gift!

But what about the times when we have to rest physically *every day*, most of the day, because we have no other choice? Rest is not always relaxing and comfortable. On the contrary, it can be irritating and painful, especially when it's a chronic pain, other health issues, or recovering from an illness or surgery. Or maybe life looks the opposite—it's a season where it's a challenge to find time for rest, even though you want to: parenting, single parenting, working more than one job to make ends meet, taking care of aging parents, or a spouse who has physical disabilities.

Because of God's mercy and compassion for us, He provides ways for us to rest in Him, even when we're struggling or life is demanding. God's gift of grace and love invites us to rest in Him.

Here's a question I'm learning to ask myself: *How many times have I turned down the invitation God gives me to experience rest in Him?*

Resting in the Lord means being in His presence. When we don't make that a habit, we become cranky restless, and we may do or say things we later regret. We can only go so long before we crash or collapse.

I once listened to Timothy Keller, a present-day theologian, preach what the Bible says about rest. Keller said there's more to us than our work and to-do list, which wears us out. What's vital to us is rest in our souls. When we don't make time for our souls to rest, we physically and mentally burn out.[2]

When reading through the Gospels, we can see how Jesus rested in rhythm—daily and weekly. As a man, Jesus experienced our core feelings, too—the need for rest is one of them. Many nights after full days of teaching, healing, standing and walking, where his body, mind, and soul needed rest. Jesus practiced Sabbath during his ministry for himself and to show his disciples and us the joy it is to rest with His Father.

Our bodies and brains need physical and mental rest; our souls need spiritual rest and rejuvenation. Rest is a gift from God. Unfortunately, we cannot see, hear, feel, or taste the goodness of rest until we figure out how to say "I'm finished" for now. As long as we can for one day each week, be finished with all you're doing, even if your to-do list still has some lines that need checking off. Be finished even if you haven't replied to all your emails. Be finished even if your home isn't clutter-free. All of that can wait.

Here are a few ways to enjoy rest:

† Listen to worship music (and go to your local church if it's the day they have a service).

† Read the Bible about God's love for you.

† Relax. Take a nap!

† Take a stroll outside. Notice the birds singing, the crunch of dried leaves, the smell of fresh air, the invisible wind brushing your face.

† Spend time with your family and/or friends over a meal. Cook your favorite food and be with people who make you laugh and help you recharge.

---

2 Timothy Keller. *Every Good Endeavor: Connecting Your Work to God's Work.* (New York: Dutton: Penguin Group, Inc. 2012)

† Do what brings you joy—a hobby, activity, or read a book for pleasure.

From experience, I know that's a challenge, but it's so worth it. When we practice sacred rhythms, we experience rest.

What a painful lesson I needed to learn. Maybe God allowed me to get shingles because He wanted me to understand what resting in Him means. During that enforced time of rest, God massaged my heart so I'd be receptive to what He was teaching me. That season taught me to rest in my soul by trusting God rather than putting my trust in myself or worldly things. God blessed me with renewed energy and deeper joy as I learned this new rhythm.

The last words written in the card I received were: "*And may you discover deep, quiet joy in the most unexpected places.*"

I say those exact words to you, friend: May *you* discover deep, quiet joy in the most unexpected places, especially while you rest.

Personal Reflections

List some of the ways you enjoy resting and relaxing. What is your Sabbath rhythm, or is that practice a struggle for you? Journal about this.

Reflect on a circumstance in your life when something unexpectantly happened that forced you to rest. How did that make you feel? Can you look back now and see how God used that time as a benefit in your spiritual growth? How?

Additional Scripture: Matthew 11:28-30, Hebrews 4:9-10, John 19:28-37

Personal Expressions

Begin or continue to practice Sabbath! Then, choose some of the ideas listed in this story and enjoy resting in the Lord!

🔊 **Listen to *Rest* by Matthew West**

Closing Prayer

Creator God, You practiced Sabbath as an example for me to rest. Your reasons and plans stand firm forever; Your intentions can never be shaken. I admit that I live in a busy world, a culture that has trouble practicing Sabbath, so please help me live with the intention to rest and desire to worship You through rest. I want to be in Your shelter, Most High, so that I can find rest in Your shadow, Almighty God. Amen.

† (Psalm 33:11, Psalm 91:1, Hebrews 4:11)

CHAPTER 27

He Sustains

Opening Prayer

May you be blessed forever, Lord, for not abandoning me when I abandoned you.

May you be blessed forever, Lord, for offering your hand of love in my darkness, most lonely moment.

May you be blessed forever, Lord for putting up with such a stubborn soul as mine.

May you be blessed forever, Lord, for loving me more than I love myself.

May you be blessed forever, Lord, for continuing to pour out your blessings upon me, even though I respond so poorly.

May you be blessed forever, Lord, for drawing out the goodness in all people, even including me.

May you be blessed forever, Lord, for repaying our sin with your love.

May you be blessed forever, Lord, for being constant and unchanging, amidst all the changes of the world.

May you be blessed forever, Lord, for your countless blessings on me and on all your creatures. Amen.

† Teresa of Avila[1]

"Restore to me the joy of your salvation and grant me the willing spirit, to sustain me." **† Psalm 51:12 (NIV)**

---

1 Teresa of Avila *The HarperCollins Book of Prayers*, comp. by Robert Van de Weyer (New York: HarperCollins Publishers, 1993) p. 349

Story

Imagine: even though the light brush of wind gently swirled around you, the April afternoon sun warms your cold, winter bones as you and your friend stand outside on the driveway. Your friend places both hands on your shoulders, look you directly in the eyes, and says these words:

"Friend, He sustained you this past year. God has been carrying you through each day and given you what you've needed—even if they were drive-through Chick-fil-a nuggets and Diet Coke. If that's what it took to get you through each day, then that's what He's let you have because that is better than you giving up hope. Because of His compassion, God has helped you get out of bed each day and do the things you've had to do. *He has sustained you.* He's carried you through your loss of a loved one, adjusting to going back to work, the reality you're about to become empty nesters, significant relational changes, and the crazy world around us. Even though you and so many other people are struggling these days, you're still hanging in there. Jesus knows and understands and will uphold you through it. Thanks be to our Lord and Sustainer!"

Have you ever felt dizzy or even sick to your stomach because it felt like you were on a bumpy roller coaster of emotions? You want the ride to be over, but it keeps moving. You want to scream, "Stop!" because it only slows down before life circumstances take another sharp turn.

If you said yes, know that you are not alone. Hopefully, as I write this, we're getting to the end of a world pandemic; it was not a joke. But it is not the only time in history, nor the future when adverse life circumstances heighten emotions, causing personal and professional struggles. People everywhere have a history of suffering. So when my heart, mind, and body are going through stressful or burdensome situations, as so many of us have experienced, I need to open the Bible to the Psalms where David wrote out his lamentations to God.

Does this ever happen to you? You'll be reading a devotion, hearing a message preached, or a song, and one particular word God wants you to pay attention to keeps reappearing? Lately, the word *sustains* keeps showing up for me, and I've discovered that word is scattered throughout the Psalms in the Bible.

The dictionary says that *sustain* means "to uphold, to keep from falling, to support, to keep from sinking, to aid, comfort and relieve." Aren't those life-saving words?

When you read through the book of Psalms, you'll see how David was not ashamed to share the emotional spectrum of how he felt about himself, others, and even God. Being a military leader, husband, father, friend, and an imperfect human after God's heart, he experienced victories and joys, but also deep distress, conflict, sin, oppression, war, depression, and stress, just like we do. He also had an enemy on his back, which does not exclude us, either.

David journaled many of his prayers to God, expressing his true feelings. Psalm 55 is a prayer where David feels alone and brokenhearted. He starts off writing,

"*Listen to my prayer, O God, do not ignore my plea; hear me and answer me. My thoughts trouble me, and I am distraught.*" Have you experienced those feelings?

David continues later in this prayer by instructing himself, and us, to "*Cast your cares on the Lord and he will sustain you.*" (55:22 NIV)

That is not the only time David expresses that promise he held tightly. In another psalm, he wrote,

> "*Restore to me the joy of your salvation and grant me the willing spirit, to sustain me.*" **(Psalm 51:12 NIV)**

> And in yet another one, "*Surely God is my help; the Lord is the one who sustains me.*" **(Psalm 54:4 NIV)**

So, how did David find hope in difficult seasons of life? As you read through many of the psalms, you'll see that he was honest with God. He told God how he truly felt, and by doing that, their relationship deepened.

Through his prayers of lament, he told God all the raw emotions he was experiencing—the good, the bad, and the ugly. David felt free to express his honest thoughts because he trusted the Lord with all his heart. David trusted that God would support him, help him, comfort him, uphold him, and even relieve him during his day-to-day life. In other words, he believed in the power of God's Spirit to sustain him. These same promises are the very ones God's Spirit has shown me during this time in history. Despite whatever is happening around us today, we can have the hope that comes from the Lord. David describes God as being a God who sustains us. We can trust that He will keep us from sinking into the mire in which we feel trapped. God relieves our stress by giving us simple joys in our day-to-day lives to notice the beauty of nature or laughter with a friend. He holds us up through our faith when we feel like throwing in the towel. He comforts us through His Word when we worry about the world caving in all around us.

In this day and age, we sometimes hear about sustainability, or sustainable development, where organizations or people strive to take care of the environment, economy, and society using natural resources. There are all types of programs and emphasis on preserving the world around us. There's even sustainable art, where artists use nature and natural materials to create beauty for the eye. There was a movement in the 1960s where artists created land art, or earth art, where things from nature were the material, and the land, or even bodies of water, were the canvas.

One summer, our family took a trip driving across the country, stopping at many National Parks, including ones in Utah. One unique thing I noticed while visiting these places was the land art, where hiking tourists (including myself) created mini sculptures made from strategically stacked stones, and twigs picked off the desert ground. They adorned the bases of the towering, weathered sandstones that God Himself had formed into works of natural art thousands of years ago.

God, our Master Creator, surely has a passion for sustainability. Sustain-ability, where He has the capability—the power—to uphold all of creation and lift the burden of our struggles, so our pressure is light. He upheld those burdens when he was upon the cross, for you and me.

He desires us to live with the assurance and freedom that He is our Sustainer. He restores the joy of our salvation to sustain us in this crazy world. To keep us from sinking and falling, He helps us by giving us a sustaining ability through His Spirit.

Modern-day Franciscan priest and teacher Richard Rohr wrote this nugget of wisdom to ponder:

"When I can stand in mystery (not knowing and not needing to know and being dazzled by such freedom), when I don't need to split, to hate, to dismiss, to compartmentalize what I cannot explain or understand... then I am beginning to stand in divine freedom (Galatians 5:1). We do not know how to stand there on our own. Someone Else needs to sustain us in such a deep and spacious place."[2]

When we're in a season filled with uncertainties, God's grace and sustaining power give us the freedom to release our struggles to Him so that we can live a hope-filled life. Thanks to David's example, he did some spiritual practices that we could implement in our daily lives to help us focus on the truth that God sustains us. I've listed them below.

† Be honest with God and tell Him how you truly feel.

† Read through the Psalms as a prayer or write a prayer to express yourself to God.

† Trust the Lord and His promises.

† Then give praise and declare, "Thanks be to our Lord and Sustainer!"

---

2 Richard Rohr. *Radical Grace: Daily Meditations by Richard Rohr* (Cincinnati, OH: St. Anthony Messenger Press, 1995)

May you never give up hope in a season of struggle when the world, or your world, feels like it's falling apart. Jesus knows and understands and will uphold you through it. Thanks be to our Lord and Sustainer!

Personal Reflections

David trusted God to sustain him through difficult times. Read the following statements, even meditate on the answers, and then fill in the blank. There's no right or wrong answer. You can ask yourself these questions whenever you want to from this day forward.

God will support me as I ....
....

God will help me ....
....

God will comfort me ....
....

God will uphold me when ....
....

God will relieve me with ....
....

Pray about a situation that overwhelms you today, using the above spiritual practices. The Holy Spirit can give you the *sustain-ability* to guide or uphold you through your trial.

Additional Scripture: Isaiah 46:3-4, Psalm 3, Hebrews 1:1-3, Psalm 55

Personal Expressions

Now it's your turn to create a piece of land or earth art. Find a place outside, for example, in your yard, a park, a wooded area, or sidewalk, and collect pieces of nature such as pebbles, rocks, acorns, leaves, twigs, sand, seashells, flowers, etc. and design a pattern or a form of sculpture using the articles you collect. Or you can even use your stirring stick and create an image with the cream or whipping cream in your cup of coffee or latte. Remember that God is your Sustainer!

🔊 **Listen to *Creator, Sustainer, Redeemer* by Emmaus**

Closing Prayer

Listen to my prayer, O God. Do not ignore my cry for help! Please listen and answer me, for I am overwhelmed by my troubles. My heart pounds in my chest. Fear and trembling overwhelm me, and I can't stop shaking. Oh, that I had wings like a dove; then I would fly away and rest! I would fly far away to the quiet of the wilderness. It feels like everything is falling apart. But I will call on You God, and You will rescue me. Morning, noon, and night I cry out in my distress, and You hear my voice. You ransom me and keep me safe from the battle waged against me. Lord, I give my burdens to You, and I believe You will take care of me. Amen. † **(parts of Psalm 55)**

CHAPTER 28

He Gives

Opening Prayer

Oh Lord, my God, I do not ask for the pain to go away. I've prayed that prayer a thousand times over, and the pain remains with me. But I'm not angry about it. I'm not ever disappointed anymore. I've come to terms with my pain. No, my prayer is much more basic, much more simple. I ask, O God, for help in getting through this day...I don't know who I am anymore, but whoever I am, Oh Lord, You know that I am Thine. Amen. † **Richard Foster** *Prayers from the Heart*[1]

"*I am worn out waiting for your rescue,*
but I have put my hope in your word.
My eyes are straining to see your promises come true.
When will you comfort me?
I am shriveled like a wineskin in the smoke,
but I have not forgotten to obey your decrees.
How long must I wait?
When will you punish those who persecute me?
These arrogant people who hate your instructions
have dug deep pits to trap me.
All your commands are trustworthy.
Protect me from those who hunt me down without cause.

---

1   Richard Foster. *Prayers from the Heart,* (San Francisco: HarperCollins Publishers, 1994)

They almost finished me off,
but I refused to abandon your commandments.
In your unfailing love, spare my life;
then I can continue to obey your laws." † **Psalm 119:81-88**

Story

Sitting on a peach-colored sofa, smelling a sweet aroma, nibbling on a Rice Krispy treat and a smoothie at a local coffee shop, my friend and I delve into a rich conversation about cheesy movies, our grown-up babies, and a pandemic because as I write this, rarely is there ever a conversation without some reference to it. In communion, we share our questions of how to grieve and desire at the same time, how conveniences and the busyness of our lives wear us down, how it feels like we're not able to have the full substance of anything anymore, and what if God's winning *feels* like our losing?

I'm honest and admit I've realized that I regularly need time alone. In solitude. I don't have to impress anyone. I won't be compared to anyone. I won't sound tongue-twisted when I try to explain something to someone. And I won't hurt anyone's ears when I sing out loud. Strangely though, my desire and longing for times of solitude can reach the point of loneliness. Sacred loneliness. The longing to be in the presence of God runs so deep I feel a holy pain—sometimes to the point of tears.

When I first felt those bone-deep emotions, I didn't know what to think. They were concerning and made me think something was wrong with me. I've known my more introverted personality proves that I need some "me time" each day, but this feeling was different. Is it okay to long to be lonely? I asked my friend that question when we sat on that soft, peach sofa. After a moment of silence, she quietly yet firmly said,

"If I didn't have loneliness, I'd be scared to soul-death."

Have you ever thought that God desires for us to feel needy—to long so deeply to be with Him? Why do you believe He created us? We are made in God's image and created to reflect who He is and how He feels. There has always been God and the Trinity, Who then formed Adam and Eve because He desired and longed for companionship. God wasn't abandoned or needy. He simply desired us.

I think there are two kinds of loneliness. There's the kind we humans feel due to an encounter of loss, isolation, or pain in our lives, and there's also the kind of loneliness where we yearn for wholeness and oneness with God that we cannot experience until we are with Him in the other side of heaven. Because of God's love and compassion for you and me, He's taught and shown us ways of living with that sacred loneliness through stories in the Bible and the examples Jesus gave us during his life on earth.

When you look at the gospels in the New Testament in the Bible, there are three main things Jesus taught the disciples by example—sharing the gospel, helping people in need, and the frequent practice of solitude for rest and prayer.

> *"Jesus traveled throughout the region of Galilee, teaching in the synagogues, and announcing the Good News about the Kingdom. And he healed every kind of disease and illness."*
>
> † **(Matthew 4:23)**

> *"Late that night, the disciples were in their boat in the middle of the lake, and Jesus was alone on land."* † **Mark 6:47**

> *"As soon as Jesus heard the news, he left in a boat to a remote area to be alone."* † **Matthew 14:13**

Jesus longed to be with His Father, our God, so he did what he could to be in communion with Him. He knew the value of being alone and in solitude. So Jesus regularly went off to be alone. When reading through the gospels, we see him praying alone. Still, there must have been times of silence, thinking, mind–wandering, remembering, dreaming, and shedding tears because of his compassion for people and his longing to be with His Father in heaven. Whatever He was doing, the essential part was that he was in solitude and silence to pay attention to God with no other distractions.

With the lack of solitude, we lack intimacy with God, and we lack needed rest and communion with the Trinity. With a lack of solitude, we lack hearing the Holy Spirit. With a lack of solitude, we become exhausted, frustrated, easily angered, empty, even desperate for something we can't name. Yet, that *something* is being in the presence of God's holiness, and it's difficult to experience that if we don't take the time to be alone with Him.

These days, it can be easy to put silence, solitude, and stillness at the bottom of our to–do list. While all these things are good, we become busy volunteering, being on committees, attending social events, and outreaches. Still, when it comes to making time for silent solitude, that's a challenge. Unless I choose to read a book about spiritual practices, rarely do I hear about the sacredness, and necessity of solitude, stillness, noiselessness, and non–distractedness, as a way to experience God and worship Him fully.

God allows us to feel the same longing Jesus had while he walked on this earth—the lonely-longing to be with his Father one day in heaven. Even though it can feel painful, lonely-longing is a gift, not a curse. It is a priceless gift to ache for God that He gives freely to anyone who longs. As you read through the Old and New Testament, you'll discover several peoples' holy longing to be with God, away from their struggles and sufferings, along with their continued obedience and respect to God; David, the king of Israel, being one of them. You can read throughout many of his psalms his true longing.

O God, you are my God;
I earnestly search for you.
My soul thirsts for you;
my whole body longs for you
in this parched and weary land
where there is no water.

I have seen you in your sanctuary and
gazed upon your power and glory.

Your unfailing love is better than life itself;
how I praise you!
I will praise you as long as I live,
lifting up my hands to you in prayer.
You satisfy me more than the richest feast.
I will praise you with songs of joy.

I lie awake thinking of you,
meditating on you through the night.
Because you are my helper,
I sing for joy in the shadow of your wings.
I cling to you;
your strong right-hand holds me securely. † **(Psalm 63:1–8)**

David's whole body—flesh, mind, and soul—longs for God just like hard, dried-up land on this earth desperately needs water to flourish. David was experiencing a deep longing to be face to face with God and His unfailing love, and nothing on this earth could fill that satisfaction. Yet, yet... while David waited for God's timing to be with Him in heaven, he chose to cling to Him, sing to Him, praise, and pray to Him and continue to point people to God.

I don't know much, but this much I know; I don't ever want to lose that lonely feeling of desire. I hope you don't want to lose that same gift God freely gives you, either.

Your desire for more of God than you have right now, your longing for love, your need for deeper levels of spiritual transformation than you have experienced so far is the truest thing about you.

Our days may be challenging. They may include strife, struggle, or surrender. So what if we consider suffering not to be a bad thing because, during those times, we often experience the nearness of God. Our unseen God is present, and we long for more of Him because we desire more of His mystery to be evident to us. It's a holy longing that is a blessing in disguise.

May our souls always hunger and thirst for God.

Personal Reflections

How often do you make time to be still, in solitude and silence? Take some time to do that. I suggest you turn your phone off or leave it in another room so that you won't be distracted by it. It doesn't have to be too long for the first time, and the more you practice this spiritual discipline, the longer the time might be. Take some deep breaths. Be in the present moment. Think about Jesus, His promises, and how God dwells in you and delights to be with you. How does it make you feel?

How can the lonely-longing be with God be a gift? Have you ever thought that God desires for you to long so deeply to be with Him? Why do you think or believe He created us?

Additional Scripture: Psalm 143:5–8, Amos 8:11, Matthew 14:22–23

Personal Expressions

Get your art supplies, magazines, newspapers, or simply a piece of paper, pencil, or marker. Create a collage of words (and pictures if you'd like) to describe your longings.

🔊 **Listen to *If I Stand* by Rich Mullins**

Closing Prayer

Almighty God, You are the Alpha and the Omega—the Beginning and the End. To all who are thirsty, You will give freely from the springs of the water of life. Lord, in the night, I search for You; in the morning, I earnestly seek You. I ponder all Your great works and think about what You have done. I lift my hands to You in prayer. I thirst for You as parched land thirsts for rain. Come quickly, Lord, and answer me, for my depression deepens. Don't turn away from me. Let me hear of Your unfailing love each morning, for I am trusting You. Show me where to walk, for I give myself to You. I long to enter the courts of the Lord with my whole being, body, and soul, and I will still shout joyfully to You, the living God. Amen

† **(Revelation 21:6, Isaiah 26:9, Psalm 73:21–26, Psalm 84:2)**

CHAPTER 29

He Asks

Opening Prayer

Thank you, Lord, that you have set eternity so firmly in my heart that no earthly thing can ever fully satisfy me. Thank you that every present joy is so mixed with sadness and unrest that it makes my mind look up to the prospect of a more perfect joy. Above all, thank you for the sure hope and promise of eternal life in your presence, which you have given me in the glorious gospel of Jesus Christ my Lord. Amen.

† **John Baillie** *A Diary of Private Prayer*[1]

The one thing I ask of the Lord—the thing I seek most—is to live in the house of the Lord all the days of my life, delighting in the Lord's perfections and meditating in his Temple. † **Psalm 27:4**

Story

You probably just asked yourself if you wanted to read a page in this book right now, and since you're reading this, your answer was "yes." You ask countless questions in your life—every decision you make each day is like asking yourself a question. "Do I hit the snooze button again, or rise and shine?" "Do I want yogurt or

---

1 John Baillie. *A Diary of Private Prayer,* (New York: Scribner: A Division of Simon & Schuster, Inc. 1949) p. 85

cereal for breakfast?" "Do I go for a walk around the block or take an afternoon nap?" Here's another question to add to your count to think about:

Have you ever asked yourself what is the first recorded question Jesus asked once he began his ministry? Having read through the four gospels, I discovered the answer to my question in John 1.

The following day John (the Baptist) was again standing with two of his disciples. As Jesus walked by, John looked at him and declared, "Look! There is the Lamb of God!" When John's two disciples heard this, they followed Jesus.

> *Jesus looked around and saw them following. "What do you want?" he asked them.* † **(John 1:35–38)**

"*What do you want?*"

In the busyness of life, how often are you asked that question, "What *do* you want?" I can imagine seeing Jesus looking directly into both Andrew and Peter's eyes and speaking to them in a way that drew them to want to leave everything they had, to follow him.

When I've asked myself that question, my answers have been to regain my complete vision, for my kids to be Christ-following adults. I want peace in this world and never any conflict—these were the first things to come to my mind. So in prayer one day, I asked God, "What do I really want, Lord?"

"Me," He said.

"Yes, I want to feel You in my life, Lord, but how can I grieve and desire at the same time? It seems like grief is smothering my desires these days."

Grieving is our reaction to loss. We've all lost someone or something in this life.

I'm learning those feelings of loss tend to reveal places of longing. There are days when it seems impossible to think of your soul's desires, much less what you're going to cook for dinner that night. But, I'm also learning that God desires intimacy with us, as well.

He designed us with a deeply embedded longing for communion. Communion is not only a sacramental practice of remembering what Jesus did on the cross for us through partaking bread and wine, but communion also means the sharing or exchanging of intimate thoughts and fellowship. It can mean an understanding and connection beyond words.

I'm just now realizing this because a few years ago, I struggled with my faith in God in a way that I never had before after twenty-plus years as a Christ-follower. I kept thinking my spiritual journey would "kick back in gear" and that God would answer my prayer, and I'd be able to connect with God as I had been for years. I'd be back into a routine of reading the Bible, participating in and leading a Bible study, volunteering, and of course, conversing with God in prayer—like it used to be—with joy and enjoyment. I kept waiting. And waiting. And waiting.

The longer I waited, the more I began to crumble. I wanted to know why my faith felt dried up and dead. I wanted to know why I began having unfamiliar feelings of pent-up agitation. Daily circumstances provoked my frustration, but mostly I was upset with myself and God because He was not making His presence known to me in the old familiar ways. This aggravation was a strange, uninvited guest, and it scared me. I was confused because my prayers seemed to be void, as though I were talking to myself. I wondered if I had lost my mind.

Yet, during what felt like a never-ending season, God's Spirit offered me a new invitation. I just didn't recognize it. I'm still trying to understand why He allowed me to struggle through that "dark night of the soul," but I can now see that God was patiently waiting for me to open the invitation He had been holding out to me for quite some time. It was an invitation to come to His table and *commune* with Him, not just *communicate* with Him. While those times with God in prayer and studying the Bible are essential, God—being the loving One He is—wanted me to draw even closer to Him in a different way.

The loss of my habitual, comfortable faith felt like a loss. A deep loss, a holy-lonely. Where had my God gone, and why had He left me alone to fend for myself? I wanted Him to come back and for our relationship to be like it used to be.

If anyone felt those feelings, it was Jesus' disciples, Jesus' mother Mary, and Mary Magdalene after Jesus died. That had to have been a long Saturday between Jesus's death and His resurrection. Distressed, huddled, and hiding in a secluded place, scared they'd be captured and crucified next, they were grieving because they witnessed their son and closest friend's violent death. They were confused because Jesus had told them he was their Savior, and he hadn't taken over the Roman government. They grappled with remembering the reasons for the warnings Jesus had given them when he had told them he would be tortured by the elders, killed, and resurrected on the third day.[2] But revisioning Jesus' broken and bloody body hanging on a cross couldn't get out of their minds, and how in the world could anyone come back to life after a death like his? They longed to be with him again as they grieved their loss.

Can grief and a desire commune together? We long for healing, wholeness, peace, joy, and rebirth in both grief and desire. Looking back now, I learned my desire was longing to be closer to Christ. Again. He had gone ahead of me to prepare a place for new and deeper intimacy; I only needed to follow Him.

Ruth Haley Barton presents this same experience so well,

> *"Your desire for more of God than you have right now, your longing for love, your need for deeper levels of spiritual*

---

2 Mark 10:43-52 (NIV)

transformation that you have experienced so far is the truest thing about you...it is your desire for God and your capacity to reach for more of God than you have right now that is the deepest essence of who you are. There is a place within each one of us that is spiritual, the place where God's Spirit witnesses with our spirit about our truest identity. Here God's Spirit dwells with our spirit, and here our truest desires make themselves known. From this place, we cry out to God for deeper union with him and with others."[3]

Are you experiencing any kind of loss that makes you feel like your soul has shrunk? Or do you sense any sort of change in your relationship with God that makes you question your faith? Is there an odd feeling of needing something, but you just can't put your finger on it? Are you in a time of change in your life that makes you feel uncomfortable? Our struggles can be part of the process of entering into a new chapter of deeper holiness and communion with God. Jesus enjoys being in our presence, and when we have that desire to be nearer to Him, we realize we need Him more and must depend on Him for everything. We can also understand that God's ways are better than the ways we think are best. The unseen work of God in our lives and this world is always more significant than we can imagine. In times of transformation, we're molded and formed into the likeness of Christ. He knows us from the inside out, and prepares a new place with new experiences, revived joy, restored peace, and a renewed life. God already knows our deep desires, even more than we do. He wants us to participate in the discovery with Him, even if it's uncomfortable.

At the beginning of this chapter, I mentioned how the first words recorded in Scripture of Jesus speaking when he first started his ministry was the question, "What do you want?"

"*What do you want?*" Jesus asks us, too.

Now, I know the answer; I want more of you, Jesus. So much more.

---

3   Ruth Haley Barton. *Sacred Rhythms: Arranging Our Lives for Spiritual Transformation,* (Illinois: InterVarsity Press, 2006) p. 24

Personal Reflections

Find a place of solitude. Take some deep breaths. Invite yourself into Jesus' presence because He's waiting for you there. Consider Jesus' question: "What do you want?" How might you answer it today, at this moment? Your response will probably not be a one-and-done deal. It's a question Jesus asks us throughout our lives. Don't be disappointed if you don't know your answer immediately. The process of coming to your answer is part of the healing, drawing you even closer to God.

The Saturday after Jesus died, all the world seemed like it was coming to an end as the disciples and women grieved and longed for Him to return. How do you hold onto hope when things feel overwhelming and impossible?

Additional Scripture: Isaiah 55, Luke 2:41–52, Acts 17:22–31

Personal Expressions

Explore how to discover and express some of your deep desires in the form of art—through music, dance, drawing, writing, or anything that lets your imagination run free. If you're not feeling particularly creative today, take a walk outside if that's where you feel closest to Him. Take a picture of that place or space so you can look back and remember it. You can even create art from the photograph if you feel led. Let yourself enjoy this holy experience.

🔊 **Listen to** *Need You Now* **by Plumb**

Closing Prayer

God, I think of You, and I am overwhelmed with longing for Your help. Help me to remember that You will give eternal life to those who keep on doing good, seeking after the glory and honor and immortality that You offer. Jesus, You said to keep on asking, and I will receive, You said to keep on seeking, and I will find, and that when I keep on knocking, the door will be opened to me. I'm going to keep asking, seeking, and knocking, Lord, seeking Your Kingdom above all else. I trust Your Word that You will give me everything I need, and that is more of You. Amen.

† (Psalm 77:3, Romans 2:7, Luke 11:9, Luke 12:31)

CHAPTER 30

Opening Prayer

Lord,
Show me the suffering of the most miserable;
So I will know my people's plight.
Free me to pray for others;
For you are present in every person.
Help me to take responsibility for my own life;
So that I can be free at last.
Give me honesty and patience;
So that I can work with other workers.
Bring forth song and celebration;
So that the Spirit will be alive among us.
Let the Spirit flourish and grow;
So that we will never tire of the struggle...

Amen

† César E. Cháv *Prayer of the Farmworkers' Struggle*[1]

---

1 César E. Chávez, UFW Founder, "Prayer of the Farm Workers' Struggle" (Los Angeles, CA: Cesar E. Chavez Foundation, 1968)

Therefore, since we have been made right in God's sight by faith, we have peace with God because of what Jesus Christ our Lord has done for us. Because of our faith, Christ has brought us into this place of undeserved privilege where we now stand, and we confidently and joyfully look forward to sharing God's glory.

† Romans 5:1–2

Story

"Life beats down and crushes the soul, and art reminds you that you have one."[2]

When I stepped into Catrina's Tequila and Taco Bar that night, I did not know what "embrace the joy while suffering" meant. But, when I left a few hours later, I did.

It had been two and a half long years.

The only longing I had was to feel, see, and hear Jesus again.

We all go through "winter" seasons in life where we feel like we've been beat down and our souls crushed: loss of a loved one, losing a job, chronic illness, a change in relationships, or feeling over-whelmed, stagnant, or stressed. Aging parents, disrespectful children, gaining weight or losing your mind, an addiction, anxiety, depression, or being abused—these are just a few situations that fall into the "soul-crushing" category.

Some winters are short, while others seem unending. God never said we would have a perfect life while living here on this blue and green ball on this side of heaven. When our good feelings become numb, unlikable feelings, they weasel their way into our souls and make themselves comfortable deep inside if you

---

2   Stella Adler, *Stella Adler on America's Master Playwrights: Eugene O'Neill, Thornton Wilder, Clifford Odets, William Saroyan, Tennessee Williams, William Inge, Arthur Miller, Edward Albee*," (New York: Vintage Books, 2012) p. 11

let them. I let them. I don't recall welcoming them in, but I also don't remember kicking them out during that difficult season.

Then there was one day. The night I went to the Taco bar. That afternoon, I connected with a friend whom I had not seen in several months. It did not take long for us to expose our bleeding hearts to each other. We were raw, telling each other our gut-honest feelings of living in what felt like dense fog and near-death hope. We talked about loss, questions and doubt, and the comfort of hiding yet suffering from loneliness. We had different grievances, but we understood how each other felt mixed-together.

When our time ran out, my friend squeezed my shoulders with her warm hands, smiled at me as she looked me in the eyes, and said, "*Today, we experienced the joy of fellowship in suffering. Embrace it.*"

Embrace the joy the Holy Spirit gives us while we're suffering. (I Thessalonians 1:6)

That same evening, I celebrated the birthday of another sweet friend with a group of close girlfriends at a Paint Nite party. Maybe you have heard of them or even participated in one? I had never been to one but had always wanted to. When I walked into the room, my heart unexpectantly skipped a beat, a smile grew on my face, and I do not think it went away until I fell asleep that night.

Even though I have a degree in Art, I didn't have much experience using paints. My specialty involved ink, charcoal, and chalk pastels. But it's not the medium that matters. It's not essential if you have a degree in art or not. It's okay if you're not a crafty person who spends most of your spending money at Hobby Lobby. That night, it was the art of simply *being*. That night was about embracing the joy the Holy Spirit gave me while I was struggling. I had not felt alive in a long time, but with a blank canvas in front of me, four paint-speckled and stained paintbrushes, and a white, Styrofoam plate with puddles of red, yellow, blue, and white acrylic paint on it, I came back to life.

The first strokes on the canvas of light blue paint for the sky made me feel like I was flying in it. Adding pale pink, pastel yellow, and white for the clouds seemed to appear magically. We were to stop painting to let the sky dry before beginning the next section of the picture, but it was hard to wait! The next instruction was to make a shade of green and start painting the grass, beginning with the brush at the bottom of the canvas, and painting upward. After that, we added yellow, orange, even blue, and purple. It was an explosion of color as the flowers popped onto the canvas.

Creating my own colors, the feel of running a brush up the canvas, watching a colorful blade of grass appear was so simple, so fulfilling. It felt like Someone was pouring the colors of happiness, hope, joy, and resurrection into my empty and blank soul.

I agree with the words of Post–Impressionist, French artist Paul Cezanne: *"A work of art which did not begin in emotion is not art."*

The field of flowers I painted was no masterpiece because, more importantly, my enthusiasm, happiness, and joy were revived. That night another Paul you may have heard about in the Bible wrote these words, *"For we are God's masterpieces. He has created us anew in Christ Jesus, so we can do the good things he planned for us long ago."* (Eph. 2:10)

I embraced every second of it and still think of that night often. Simply being with friends, given a blank canvas and some paint, helped me remember that joy exists even in the bleak days of winter. That evening in Catrina's Tequila and Taco Bar, I came back to life in a makeshift art studio. As I fell asleep that night, the words spoken to me earlier that day sang in my mind: *Today, we experienced the joy of fellowship in suffering. Embrace it."*

Now I say this to you today, my reading friend: Embrace the joy the Holy Spirit gives *you* when you're struggling or suffering. That instruction comes from God's Word:

> *Embrace how Jesus, who for the joy that was set before him, endured the cross.* † **(Hebrews 12:2)**

> *Embrace how we can share abundantly in Christ's suffering, so through him, we can share abundantly in comfort, too.*
>
> † **(2 Corinthians 1:5)**

We're to imitate Christ, and He embraced and endured as we see in the Scripture just read. Embrace means to surround or encircle oneself. Endure means to suffer patiently. As Jesus-followers, we're to surround ourselves with how he patiently suffered the cross with joy *that was set before him*. We're to surround ourselves with how Jesus patiently suffered on the cross with joy *that is set before us, too.*

We're not promised or even told that life will no longer be hard once we become Christ-followers, and all our struggles and suffering will go away. Suffering is part of becoming like Christ—and Christ suffered—all for the joy that awaits us in heaven for eternity. Here, in this life, we have times of great sorrow, and we have times of great joy. And that's okay and normal.

Author K.J. Ramsey, in her soul-stirring book *This Too Shall Last,* writes this certainty:

> *"Suffering is a place we will repeatedly find ourselves in as we journey toward the wholeness God has for us in his kingdom. Whether we try to escape it or pretend we aren't there, suffering is a place we will repeatedly occupy as we await the return of Jesus and the restoration he will bring."*

She continues to say,

> *"Suffering does not have to be a barrier. It can be a continual reminder that there is no part of your life where Christ is not present. There is no place too low for him to stoop down. There is no part of your body too inconvenient for him to love. There is no place in your memory too dark for him to hold. There is no recurring weakness too strong for Christ to intercede. He is patient, and he is present. Christ is holding us together by the power of his Spirit, wrapping scarred hands securely around the most shattered pieces of our stories, carrying them with care because he chose to be shattered first, and placing them perfectly alongside his own into a mosaic of glory."[3]*

Recall above Paul's words that we are God's masterpieces. *What if the masterpiece is a beautiful mosaic of our suffering* because God causes each broken piece to work together for good?[4] Because of the joy of his promised renewed life to come, Jesus was able to endure the suffering on the cross. When suffering, because of Christ, we're able to endure great sorrows and struggles and embrace them with deep, great joy. Joy is a holy feeling, unlike happiness which we wish more often. Happiness can be temporary. Joy is forever in the presence of God, which we can experience even now in the midst of suffering.

May you not endure the struggling alone, but with Christ. May you embrace the joy the Holy Spirit gives you while you're struggling—when you're feeling discouraged, when you're hurting, when you're uncertain about the future, questioning your purpose, or not hearing God's voice or feeling His presence. May you still cling tightly to Jesus never letting go. May you dig deeper into the Gospel, so you'll know His overflowing compassion for you. May you know God is with you in the light and the dark spaces of life. And may you believe that *you*, my friend, are His breathtaking and beautiful masterpiece that He absolutely adores.

Amen.

---

3   K.J. Ramsey. *This Too Shall Last: Finding Grace When Suffering Lingers*, (Grand Rapids, MI: Zondervan Reflective, 2020) p. 101
4   Romans 8:28

Personal Reflections

Reflect on your own "winter" seasons. Name the times when embracing suffering has felt too difficult. Does the idea of "embracing suffering" make you wince or want to run and hide? Are you willing to learn the art of suffering?

After reading the suggested Scripture verses, what are Paul's teachings about suffering? How do they make you feel?

Additional Scripture: Philippians 3:10–14, 2 Corinthians 11:22–33

Personal Expressions

What is one of your favorite hands-on, past-time activities? Adult coloring books, doodling, writing a song or poem, digging in the dirt, building something, playing an instrument, asking a friend to play tennis? Do that this week. Find an hour in your schedule to do that activity and make an appointment for yourself in your calendar. Afterward, reflect on how it felt to do something that brought you joy.

🔊 **Listen to the hymn** *How Great Thou Art*

Closing Prayer

Abba, Father, Thank You for adopting me as Your child to be an heir of Your glory. Help me to remember that nothing compares to the glory You will reveal to me later as I go through struggles now. Thank You for declaring and teaching me to embrace the gift You've given me to share abundantly in Christ's suffering, so through Him, I can share abundantly in Your comfort, too.

You the One Who created me anew in Christ Jesus, so I can do the good things You planned for me long ago. My soul and love want never to give up, never lose faith, be hopeful in You, and endure through every circumstance for Your glory. Thank You for the gift to be. To be Your beloved. In Jesus's name, Amen.

† **(Romans 8:15–18, 2 Corinthians 1:5, Ephesians 3:9, 1 Corinthians 13:7, Song of Solomon 5:1)**

Appendix: Personal Expressions

Chapter 21: Pray Anyway—Acrylic Pouring Project

This project does take several steps and requires some unique art supplies you'll need to get before doing this project, but ANYBODY can do this! Once you purchase the supplies, they can be used for several projects to do again in the future. This activity is also fun to create with other people of all ages—10 and up.

You'll need:

  † a canvas (8x10 or larger, not flat, and wiped with a clean towel)

  † 4 different acrylic paint colors of your choice

  † white semi-gloss paint

  † 8oz or more regular glue

  † floetrol (you can get it on Amazon or craft stores)

  † cardboard larger than your canvas

  † newspaper or plastic lining

  † silicone oil (found on Amazon or in the paint department of craft stores)

  † popsicle sticks

  † 6 clear plastic cups

  † 4 pushpins

  † a hairdryer

  † gloves (optional because this can be a little messy!)

Read all the instructions before beginning the activity!

Cover a table with newspaper or plastic.

Place a piece of cardboard larger than your canvas on the table.

Turn your canvas upside down and put pushpins in each canvas corner to lift it off the cardboard. Doing this prevents the paint from sticking to the cardboard as it dries.

In each cup, pour enough floetrol to cover the bottom of the cup, then add a little more.

Now pour the same amount of regular glue on top of the floetrol in each cup.

Add a popsicle stick into each cup and stir the mixture well.

Add a pretty big quirt (a little less than the amount you used for the glue) of one color of paint in each cup. Now stir each cup well. It's OK if some are a little thicker or thinner consistency. It's actually good to have different consistencies, so if you want to thin one of the paint colors, add a few drops of water.

Add 3 tiny drops of silicone in 4 of the colors (including white)

Take the stir stick in each cup and stir it around 1, 2, 3 times.

Take the empty plastic cup and pour white paint mixture until it covers the bottom of the cup, and then pour for a few more seconds. Then take a darker color and add a little less paint than white. Then take a lighter color paint and pour a slightly less over the darker color. Do this until you add all colors. Then repeat each step starting with white and again adding all colors. (You don't have to finish all the paint in the cup)

Take another popsicle stick, put it in the cup with all the paint colors, and move the stick in a crisscross motion, as if you're making the shape of a cross. Do not remove the stick from the paint when you make this motion, and do it only once. Then, remove the stick from the cup.

Now it's time to pour! You can start wherever you'd like on the canvas—a corner, the middle, or wherever! Move the paint around the canvas as you pour most of it on the canvas. It does not need to cover the entire canvas; it's actually good to leave some negative (blank) space.

Pick up the canvas and begin tilting it around to allow the paint to run over to places you left free of color. It's OK if paint rolls over the sides of the canvas. You can leave some negative space without paint if you'd like. This time is for you to be creative and watch it flow! If you'd like, you can add the rest of your paint mixture to the canvas and tilt it around as well.

Now take the hairdryer and get it close enough to the canvas that it pushes the paint when you turn it on. Do this in the right and left motion quickly as you see cells pop out due to the silicone for about 5- 10 seconds.

If you'd like to, you can repeat steps 11–15 with the paint remaining in each of the cups. Let your creative juices flow. You can add more of a particular color or two or three more colors.

When you're finished painting, let it dry as much as possible before moving it to a different location to finish drying. You can pick up the cardboard with the canvas on it and put it on a flat surface so the paint doesn't run anymore. Let it dry overnight or at least 24 hours because the paint on the canvas is thick.

Have fun! You can find plenty of examples on YouTube—just type in "Acrylic Pouring."

(The cover of this book is an acrylic pouring piece I created)

(If you want to watch instructions for either of these activities, you can easily find them on the internet if you search for "Easy Acrylic Paining" or "Rubber Band Art Projects")

Chapter 22: Go to a Counselor—Rubber Band Resist art project.

You'll need:

- † a sponge

- † a piece of cardboard (half the size of the paper you use)

- † white cardstock or watercolor paper

- † several rubber bands (different widths are great but not required)

- † shallow plastic container to mix colors

- † liquid watercolors (pretty inexpensive on Amazon or craft stores)

Fold one sheet of paper around your cardboard.

Start wrapping rubber bands around the paper to create a pattern of lines. The more bands, the better!

Combine liquid watercolor paint with a little bit of water in a shallow container.

Dab the sponge in the paint, squeezing out a little excess water but not all of it, then gently press the sponge on your paper and overtop the rubber bands. You can use one color or use several. Don't press the sponge down too hard because that will cause the paint to run under the rubber bands and will lose the resistance to create the design.

Turn the paper over and repeat Step 4 on the other side.

Allow the paint to dry. Once dry, remove the rubber bands and open the artwork you created, seeing the resist effect.

Acknowledgments

Thank-full. That's how I feel. As I've written this book, my cup has run over with the encouragement, support, help, and love that people have given me through this journey.

Scott – I would not have written without the affirmation you gave me long before I ever started writing it, and you still do. Thank you for loving me so well through this journey. I love you.

My family – Thank you for loving me constantly in the ups and downs of life and in the middle, too. My gratitude and love for your constant support are a treasure I will always hold onto tightly. I love you, too.

Kris Camealy – Thank you for the many hours you spent reading this project as you edited my work. I cannot thank you enough for your excellent work and the spiritual guidance you've given me.

Nelly Murariu – Thank you for making my book come alive with your formatting design! You are so talented at what you do and I'm so grateful for your patience with me and your creative work.

The Flourish Writers (FW) Founders, Mindy Kiker and Jenny Kochert – Thank you for creating the community of writers and the opportunity to learn more about the craft of writing. Thank you for the one-on-one coaching calls, emails, and courses you taught, and especially for making Jesus the center of it all.

My FW Mastermind group: Marvita, Jenni, Jennifer, Melissa, and Tammy – You prayed over me and for me, along with pushing me to commit to this project that had been on my heart for years. I still get teary-eyed when I think of that one Zoom meeting that became my turning point to pursue this passion. Thank you for making our many conversations a safe place to dream and helping me make one come true. I'm so grateful to all of you.

Melissa – Your coaching calls and goal-setting skills were a gift to me. TAOS might not have been published if it weren't for your guidance and encouragement.

My dear friends – You know who you are because you prayed for me knowing I needed it, you've pushed me to keep going when I felt like giving up, and you reminded me why I was writing this. I don't deserve to have so many of you to cheer me on through this process. Thank you from the bottom of my heart.

God, Jesus, and the Holy Spirit – Someone once told me, "Pick up your pen because HE can move it." And that, HE has done. Writing TAOS has not been an easy process. The experiences I wrote about I do not boast about, and I still feel uncomfortable letting others know about them. I want to be completely healed on this side of heaven, but God has taught me there *is* an art to struggling—and that is to struggle well. The only way to do that is to depend on Him desperately. Life's struggles do not appear to be beautiful pictures by themselves, but God has shown me that they will all be part of the breathtaking masterpiece He will reveal to us the day we see Jesus face to face. Thank you, Lord, for being patient with me, for Your grace and mercy, for guiding my mind and hand as I wrote TAOS, and for filling my soul with just what it needed. Thank You for putting this desire in my heart since I was a child and making it happen for such a time as this. I love you deeply.

About the Author

Beth Hildebrand is a writer, blogger, mentor, and leader in her church and community. She lives in North Carolina with her husband, has a son and daughter in college, and enjoys traveling, several forms of art, reading, and dancing with friends whenever there's a chance.

You can find her on her **website:** www.BethHildebrand.com,
Instagram: @bethnhildebrand_author, and
Facebook: Beth Hildebrand, Author.

Made in the USA
Columbia, SC
01 February 2023

11352056R00141